ON THE BATTLEFIELD

Overcoming Challenges Associated with the Aftermath of Military Experiences

© 2019 Constance C. Cotton

All rights reserved. No part of this publication may be reproduced, distributed, or transmitted in any form or by any means, including photocopying, recording, or other electronic or mechanical methods, without the prior written permission of the publisher, except in the case of brief quotations embodied in critical reviews and certain other noncommercial uses permitted by copyright law.

ISBN: 978-17938707-4-2

SBG MEDIA GROUP AND PUBLISHING

www.thescatterbrainedgenius.com/publishing

ON THE BATTLEFIELD

BATTLEFIELD

Overcoming Challenges Associated with the
Aftermath of Military Experiences

CONSTANCE C. COTTON

FOREWORD

You will call, and I will answer;
You will cry for help, and He will say, Here I am.

(Isaiah 58:9)

I was victim to unquestionable wrongdoings and undesirable sexual encounters while serving on and off the battlefield. However, my education and spiritual growth showed me that self-esteem plays an important role in my ability to endure the fear of retribution and stressful humiliation as I recover from traumatic and challenging encounters.

God kept Constance Cotton and so many of us *ALIVE*. God did this so we could share our stories with others, in the hope that they too could find peace and purpose in our Battle Sister's pain while indulging in His presence.

As Christ-like "women veterans" we choose **GOD** our Father just like Abraham did.

Knowing that, He's our Godhead.

And as our Godhead also, known as our Father,

He is ruler of the entire universe.
His will is achieved through His Spirit.
He is all-powerful and possesses all authority.
He is the very meaning of *LOVE* and has a perfect righteous character.
He sent His son Jesus, in the form of a human to reveal His *LOVE, GRACE,* and *PLAN* for each of us. Yes, you too **Woman Veteran**!

Scriptural Readings: Matthew 11:27; John 1:1 - 2, 17 - 18, 6:44, 8:16 - 18, 14:28, 16:27; 1 John 4:8, 16; 1 Corinthians 15:24 - 28; Ephesians 3:14 - 19, 4:4 - 6; Hebrews 1:1 - 2; 2:3 - 9; Revelation 21:22

Whether on or off the battlefield,
We no longer look down; we *CHOOSE* to look up.
Constance Cotton has been blessed by the Holy Spirit to graciously break the silence of deep-rooted secrets and pain that we as veterans have bottled-up for centuries for fear of retaliation and condemnation. Constance does an amazing job conveying our emotions and our silent cry for help.

As **Women Veterans** "We See Each Other!"

I hope sister comrades are encouraged by Philippians 1:18-21 which says "Yes, and I will continue to rejoice, for I know that through your prayers and God's provision of the Spirit of Jesus Christ what has happened to me will turn out for my deliverance. I eagerly expect and hope that I will in no way be ashamed but will have enough courage so that now as always Christ will be exalted in my body, whether by life or by death. For to me, to live is Christ and to die is gain." (New International Version)

Dr. Betty Burroughs Speaks

LIC#81261 Exp 3/2/24

THE MISSION

"On the Battlefield" portrays the journeys of women veterans and the spiritual paths that have helped them in different ways. *"On the Battlefield"* breaks the silence about the struggles and suffering women veterans endure. *"On the Battlefield"* ushers readers into the lives of women veterans and their families and dismisses some misconceptions about women who served in the military. *"On the Battlefield"* reveals the hidden and overlooked challenges of women who fought for this country's freedom and presents spiritual opportunities to help them heal.

ACKNOWLEDGEMENTS

This book is a result of the grace, mercy, and love bestowed upon me by God. Thank you, Dr. Marilyn E. Porter, for publishing my book.

Thank you to my loving husband and sons for your unconditional love, sacrifices, patience, and support especially through my seminary journey.

Thank you to my parents for giving me a solid foundation built on love, faith, and acceptance.

Thank you to my sister for your ongoing support, love, and concern for our family.

I'm thankful for the mental health counselors especially Renee that gave me a safe place to do my inner work. Thank you for allowing me to be vulnerable and learn the importance of self-love and healing.

Thank you to the courageous women veterans

and special people for their contributions to this book by sharing your stories and time. Thank you Dafina for editing my first book. Thank you, Mimi, for your friendship and introducing me to Laura Lee, who was instrumental in helping me make important changes to this book, so it could be republished. Thank you, Laura Lee, for your compassion, expertise, and hard work.

Thank you to Enon Tabernacle Baptist Church and the other faith-based organizations for your prayers and encouragement.

I'm grateful to the students, faculty, and staff at The Lutheran Theological Seminary at Philadelphia for providing an inclusive and affirming community which helped me grow spiritually and cultivate more hope.
Thank you, Charles R. Leonard, who also served in the military, for mentoring me as my academic advisor and giving me the idea to create this book.

INTRODUCTION

Like so many before me, and I am sure many after me, I belong to an elite group of selfless people who is categorized as veterans. I earned the right to join the ranks of the United States veterans. After separating from the military, I was given a folder filled with paperwork which verifies that I qualified to be called a veteran – and yes, I am grateful for the opportunity I had to serve my country. I have no regrets about being in the military.

Here are a few facts about our veteran status:

- The status of our discharge will determine the benefits that are accessible to us.

- The Veterans Administration (VA) is the primary organization that provides our medical care and other pertinent resources for us; they are obtainable based on whether we served in peacetime or war.

- We must apply for our benefits to obtain care from the VA. Over the years, especially after the Desert Storm, Iraq, and Afghanistan Wars, veteran benefits have been delayed by the Veterans Administration due to a backlog of claims, bogus appointments, and medical care denials.

Here are my ideas based on my needs as a veteran:

- Veterans and their families need support and resources to help them cope with transitioning back into society.

- Veterans need safe spaces and places to grow spiritually. They need to discuss their personal needs and challenges, which can aid with their healing journey.

- Veterans should have opportunities to tell their stories, so people can understand them better.

- Faith organizations should create a veterans ministry to help us transition back into society.

As military veterans we deserve the best care and resources available to us. We veterans have willingly sacrificed our lives and relationships to ensure the freedom and safety of the United States of America – America the Beautiful, land of the free and home of the brave. Let me be clear on who veterans are; we have served in the Army, Air Force, Navy, Marines, and Coast Guard. We held duty positions during peacetime and war. Even if we were drafted, we contributed to America's freedom.

Many of us worked in hazardous and dangerous environments, while others served in combat zones. Regardless of the location or position of our jobs – we served! Because of the perils and life-threatening environments of the combat zones, many of us suffer from mental and physical problems that require access to continuous and upstanding medical care by well-trained doctors in state -of -the- art medical facilities. Unfortunately, this is not always the case. The VA was established to provide us with this care, but sadly, many of us veterans – who so freely gave their lives for the sake of others' lives – are denied benefits and resources. The VA is the foremost source for medical care, housing, education, and life insurance benefits for veterans. The VA also has the responsibility to connect veterans to an array of resources; yet many veterans are suffering from high rates of unemployment, homelessness, alcohol and substance abuse, and incarceration. I include myself as one who has experienced more than one of these misfortunes.

I know most of you are familiar with Post-Traumatic Stress Disorder (PTSD). It is perhaps most commonly known among civilians; however, veterans, suffer from it due to the circumstances of their service. Veterans also struggle with the effects of military sexual trauma (MST), Traumatic Brain Injury (TBI), and let's not leave out the soul and moral injury that comes with serving in the military. Because of these and other factors, suicide rates among veterans are extremely elevated; some studies show that 18-22 veterans commit suicide daily. I am also deeply saddened to tell you that these rates are now rising in active military members as well.

The soul trauma and the moral trauma are the issues that go uncared for in many of us. The truth is that veterans and their families need help. Faith organizations can assist them by establishing ministries which can help alleviate some of their suffering. Ministries which are trained and committed to the soul recovery of veterans can provide a safe place for veteran communities to share their stories, so others can better understand them. These ministries could also provide a sacred space for veterans and their families to heal, share resources, develop relationships, and establish a supportive community. I am a spiritual person and I know that my faith in God has tremendously helped my healing process.

I am a woman, I am a mother, I am child of God, and I am a veteran, and I know that all areas of my existence needed to be healed after military service to my country. More than anything, my soul was broken, and my body harmed.

TABLE OF CONTENTS

THE MISSION	vii
ACKNOWLEDGEMENTS	viii
INTRODUCTION	x
SILENT SCREAM	xvii
COMING HOME	19
SISTER VETERANS OF FAITH	37
FAMILIES	100
BACK TO THE VETERANS ADMINISTRATION	118
MY JOURNEY TO RESILIENCE	135
IN MY OWN WORDS	154
SUPPORTING VETERANS	193
RESOURCES	212
Bibliography	215
ABOUT THE AUTHOR	218

SILENT SCREAM

You cannot see a Silent Scream

When looking from outside.

But you might find a glimpse of it

While peering deep in someone's eyes.

You will not hear a Silent Scream

In noisy, crowded rooms.

But if you sat down face to face

Your heart may sense its painful tune.

You shall not feel a Silent Scream

Amidst our fast-paced world.

But if you wandered near to it

Its anxious spirit might unfurl.

We walk right past a suffering soul

And often turn away.

Not strong enough to face the grief

This world has made them pay.

For Silent Screams are not unique

To those who fight and die.

The living warrior hell survived

Is left to hold his tears inside.

Janet J. Seahorn, Ph.D

COMING HOME

My name is Constance C. Cotton. In August of 2004, I became a retired disabled war veteran after serving 17 years in the Army. I want to formally introduce myself to you and take you on my journey to becoming a veteran.

My Story:

While in the military, the Army Reserves in Pennsylvania was my primary duty assignment for six years. I was on active duty for 11 years before being medically retired due to disabilities incurred during Desert Shield/Desert Storm, also known as the Persian Gulf War, or the First Iraq War. Being a part of the military was one of the best decisions for me, and I have no regrets. My father served during the Korean War era, and I was so intrigued by the Army stories he shared with me that as he described his military experience, I knew I wanted to join the Army.

My grooming to serve my country also came from attending a boarding school named Scotland School for Veterans' Children (SSVC) in Scotland, PA, from sixth to twelfth grade. SSVC provided a top-notch education and resources for children of military veterans since 1895. Most students came from Philadelphia, PA, which is where I lived prior to attending. Students at SSVC were required to participate in JROTC from 9th-12th grade; my interest in the military grew as I advanced through the ranks. SSVC provided a safe, caring, and supportive environment for me, which gave me a strong community to thrive in.

After high school students returned to their homes, and my family remained in Philadelphia. My adjustment to city life was difficult, because we lived in an impoverished community with high crime rates and no community support. Finding a decent job was challenging, so my decision to join the military became easier. Adventure, traveling, earning an income, being independent, and getting away from home were very appealing to me. I joined the military in 1988.

The Army Reserves allowed me to get specialized job training and opportunities to travel throughout the United States and overseas. My job was in the medical field and I really liked it. While in the Army Reserves, soldiers were required to work one weekend a month and two weeks in the summer, and we were given special duty assignments as well. As a civilian, I worked as a package car driver at United Parcel Service (UPS); that was a hard job because it required a lot of heavy lifting, as well as timed deliveries and pickups. For some reason, male- dominated jobs interested me.

In November of 1990, my Army Reserve unit was activated during Desert Shield to go to Saudi Arabia. We couldn't believe it. For the first time, many Army Reserve units were called upon to defend Saudi Arabia with coalition military forces from August 1990 to January 1991. The military made it mandatory for us to receive anthrax vaccinations and take anti-nerve agent pills called pyridostigmine bromide. Soldiers, including myself, started to get sick shortly thereafter. We also had many challenges with enduring the sandstorms, toxic environments, and extreme heat.

During our time there, Desert Shield became Desert Storm after George H. W. Bush declared war. My unit was stationed in Dhahran, Saudi

Arabia. We were close by the Pennsylvania unit that was attacked by a scud missile; 27 soldiers died. We were devastated. We moved to Riyadh to support another unit and we often endured scud missile attacks. The effects of war took a toll on me; I dealt with medical problems and missing my family. After the war ceased, my unit returned home, and we were required to have a medical physical. The medical personnel documented my conditions, illnesses, and symptoms. Afterwards, we returned home to our families.

My father picked me up from the Army Reserve unit. Later that day, he told me that I was acting differently and that he was concerned about me. Life seemed strange. It was hard for me to sleep, my family was irritating me, my desire to have fun was diminished, and I had a hard time adjusting to being home. United Parcel Service (UPS) welcomed me home, but doing my job was difficult, and my health started to deteriorate. Enlisting full time in the Army was the best recourse at the time because it was familiar, and they provided necessary benefits, but my experience in Desert Storm started to affect me at home. When I drove across bridges, anxiety would overwhelm me and made me sweat profusely. I wanted to drive off the bridge. My trust for people lessened, and when in public, crowds scared me. Relationships with some friends and family became estranged, and people commented about my anger and changed behaviors. My life was not the same. People misunderstood me, but very few people took the time to ask me what happened during my time in the war. I wanted to share my story so that people could understand me better. Instead, I told people that I was a war veteran, just in case I have a Post-Traumatic Stress Disorder (PTSD) symptom, or a medical situation happened.

As time went by, I married a great guy and gave birth to two wonderful boys, yet my struggles continued even though I had a good support system. I still felt misunderstood and it was difficult for me to articulate what I was feeling. At times, committing suicide seemed like a good option because I was tired of being in emotional and physical pain. Mental health providers diagnosed me with PTSD, depression, and anxiety. Doctors at a military hospital diagnosed me with many medical problems, including Gulf War Illness (GWI). The Army medically retired me as a permanently disabled veteran at 37 years old. Since childhood, I have had a relationship with God, and He has helped and kept me. I have felt God's call in my life for years. In 2012, God gave me the opportunity to attend seminary. I started at Palmer Theological Seminary and graduated from Lutheran Theological Seminary in Philadelphia (LTSP). From seminary training to military-related events, God has blessed me with great knowledge to get the help I need, and I feel called to help others. My seminary journey has taken four years, yet I have gained healing, understanding and insight that have positively changed my life.

Like many veterans, especially those who fought in wars, assimilating back into society was difficult. The military trains service members to conform to the military lifestyle and fight in wars. However, once they leave, no one shows them how to be a civilian again. In some ways, the military can institutionalize people; once they become veterans, it's hard to function in society. Unfortunately, many veterans must fight for their benefits from the VA. Veterans have to wait for various timeframes to receive their benefits, if approved. In the meantime, veterans endure high unemployment rates, homelessness, high incarceration rates, and lack of mental and medical care. Some veterans can adjust back into society, but a significant number have trouble doing so.

Over the years, I have spoken to many veterans who each feel like "a fish out of water" when it comes to being in and functioning in society. Some have shared that they miss being in a military community with resources and like-minded people, while others face an identity crisis. Subsequently, their veteran status has caused them to grieve as they deal with isolation, drug and alcohol problems, and mental health problems. They feel misunderstood, and I can relate to many veterans' stories that surround those challenges.

I desired to seek the needed help and the opportunity to attend seminary brought me healing. My faith and relationship with God that began as a child has assisted me with navigating life. As I reflect on how on the years at seminary helped me to heal, I see that the veterans I met along the way, and the resources and events available to me, assisted me. I gained insight and understanding about veterans' life challenges, and today my prayer is that this book will help readers show compassion and care towards veterans. Also, I hope it will help readers to better understand veterans, especially women war veterans, and assist with providing spaces and places that foster healing, community, and integration back into society.

Veterans, especially women veterans, need opportunities to tell their stories so others can understand who they are, what they did and endured in the military, and what it's like to be a veteran. Some people tend to make assumptions about what military life entails, or what a veteran is, which lead to misconceptions and false, preconceived notions. On the contrary, other people may not know much about the military or veterans. Recently, in an article titled "First Lady to Women Veterans: 'Tell Your Story'", Michelle Obama said, "The striking reality is that those women in uniform and 3 million living women veterans still face plenty of challenges as they serve this country and then transition back to civilian life."[1]

Unfortunately, women veterans' stories, statistics, and problems tend to be excluded in the media and in mainstream dialogue. One of my favorite books is *When Jane Comes Marching Home: Portraits of Women Combat Veterans*, by Laura Browder. The book has pictures and stories of women combat veterans that exemplify their varied experiences in the military. The book has helped me realize that I am not alone. I appreciate these women's service, sacrifice, and resilience. Over the years, I have given women war veterans a copy of the book to hopefully inspire them. Adjusting to life as a female veteran, especially after combat, can feel like an

---

[1] Parrish, Karen. "First Lady to Women Veterans: "Tell Your Story" http//www.defense.gov, (accessed March 2, 2016)

uphill battle. Loved ones may not realize that you're not the same person to them- or yourself- and it's hard to articulate the change. Some women veterans that were assigned to the medical units were responsible for handling wounded service members and their body parts, disfigured patients, and deceased military personnel in large numbers. Those medical units including military hospitals were not located in the war zones. The medical personnel involved, even though they're considered to be noncombatants, have been diagnosed with PTSD and other mental health conditions as well as physical ailments like war veterans. In the book, it mentions that "Some feel they are still at war, except the battles they are fighting are within themselves and they have become their own enemy."² To add insult to injury, female veterans must fight for respect and recognition.

My military career contains many examples of racism, sexism, and infractions done to me. One time I was applying for a benefit specifically for war veterans, and the person in charge of approving my paperwork denied me the benefit. He questioned my actual participation in a combat zone, even though my DD 214 and a letter from the VA verified that I was a disabled war veteran. I was furious. I had to get other people involved to fight his decision, and the incident was a big trigger for me. The man and his boss invited me to a meeting, so I could prove that I was stationed in a combat zone. For a while in the meeting, I just expressed my

---

² Laura Browder. *When Janey Comes Marching Home: Portraits of Women Combat Veterans.* (North Carolina: University of North Carolina Press, 2010), 76.

frustration when they told me that my benefit was still denied.

After that, I called my senator and others to assist me. I was referred to a well- known white man who worked for The Department of Veterans Affairs to discuss my problem. He telephoned the boss of the man who denied me my benefit and informed him that my documentation was accurate, and the medals listed on my DD 214 showed my participation in actual combat. I believe to this day racism and sexism were a part of that denial. I had to prove my status of being a female war vet to older male war veterans. Since I qualified, I decided to join the Veterans of Foreign Wars (VFW) so I could develop relationships with other war veterans and serve my community. I served as a service officer in two VFW's, where I was the only female in both and the only African American in one of them. Both VFW's had members who felt very uncomfortable with my being a member and clearly expressed their dissatisfaction. One of the VFW's had members contest my membership because they didn't think I served in combat. Also, they strongly suggested that I work with and join the Ladies Auxiliary at the VFW Post. I stopped attending the meetings and let my membership expire at both VFW's.

Life as a female war veteran can be full of struggles, mistreatment by others, and disrespect. Many times, we are misunderstood and may feel lonely and isolated. Acceptance, restoration, and hope can help veterans, particularly women veterans, assimilate more easily because these things give us opportunities to heal. Establishing relationships in supportive communities that address our issues and giving us chances to interact with other veterans can inspire us to live productive, healthy, and meaningful lives. Veterans need a lot of support and guidance, because:

> In the military, they were taught to fight, to rush into battle expecting hostility. The soldiers were taught how to shoot a gun, how to identify and overcome the enemy, secure an area, and dismantle the target. They were never taught how to deal with the aftermath of battle. They were never told about the price they would pay for killing and viewing death firsthand. And they were never taught how to return to civilian life as though nothing had changed.[3]

---

[3] Janet J. Seahorn, and E. Anthony Seahorn. *Tears of a Warrior: A Family's Story of Combat and Living with PTSD.* (Colorado: Team Pursuits, 2008), 155-156.

SISTER VETERANS OF FAITH

The following chapter contains interviews I conducted with women veterans. It reveals their experiences, strength, and spirituality. I am so thankful to God for allowing me to meet and have a relationship with the women veterans I interviewed here.

AVERY JOHNSON

In 2012, I met Avery Johnson at a military event downtown in Philadelphia, Pennsylvania. A female war veteran was taking photographs of war veterans for a book she was creating. Avery and I were the only females present for pictures and we introduced ourselves. Avery and I have attended several women veteran events since then and we keep in touch.

What branch of the service were you in and how long did you serve in the military?

Avery: I served in the United States Air Force Reserve from May 1976 to June 2009 at the 514th Air Mobility Wing. Then I was in the Air National Guard from June 2009 to January 2012 with the 177th Fighter Wing.

What was your military occupation and what were your duties?

Avery: From 1976 to 1998, I served as an Avionics Navigation Technician. My responsibilities included: maintenance of altimeters, radars, tacans, glide scopes, aircraft black boxes, and antennae for C141 cargo aircraft. I was assigned to McGuire AFB and we were responsible for cargo planes flying to the east coast and Europe.

From 1998 to 2012, I was a Chaplain Assistant. My responsibilities included administration, religious services, programs, troop morale, and security for the Chaplain. After my promotion to MSgt, I became a Program Manager and Supervisor.

Did you serve in any combat zones? If so, where?

Avery: Yes; I was stationed at Kuwait, Ali Asalem, from December 2005 to May 2006, and Camp Cunningham, Afghanistan, from December 2007 to May 2008

What were some of the challenges you faced in the military?

Avery: I was 24 when I joined the military. I always say my first experience with the military was like the movie "Private Benjamin." The recruiter sold me a bill of goods and I received a reality check my first week of Basic Training. Three days into training I recognized it was a psychological game, and I decided nothing would get in the way of my graduating from Boot Camp on time.

I arrived at Kessler AFB in October of 1976, reported to class, and found out I was in a predominantly male career field for electronics, and not in the computer course that I had expected to be in. A Sergeant in my class told me women should be at home barefoot and pregnant. Out of a starting class of 14 men and 1 female, I was 1 of 9 to graduate. The Sergeant washed out of the program. I spent a lot of time in remedial studies during the program and had an instructor who made attempts at sexual harassment. I reported him immediately.

Reporting to my shop at McGuire AFB was a culture shock. Redneck white males tried to control me by intimidation. By the end of my 1st enlistment I decided I would quit. The powers that be called me into a meeting and told me I would not be able to reenlist. That action motivated me to fight back! I filed a case with the Senior Enlisted Advisor that resulted in my getting a promotion and reenlisting for 6 years. There was no negative documentation in my records. My Unit had a party, and female strippers performed. I confronted my Commander about having female strippers at our Christmas party with women in the unit. That was the last year for strippers. I worked for a wing Chaplain who was intimidating and jealous of my male friends who stopped by our office to see me.

I did three tours to the port mortuary. During that time, the challenging situations were difficult for me. I heard a counseling session wherein a person was not released to attend his grandmother's funeral because she was not listed as immediate family; however, she was the person who raised him. I read "Dear John" letters received by military members while deployed, and someone told me one woman recipient was considering suicide. A woman told me she was raped, but she was unwilling to testify. I was struggling with the decision to deploy, considering the possible effect on my career from my civilian employer, and I was living with the politics of military life.

How has your faith helped you throughout your life and especially as a veteran?

Avery: My faith has helped me throughout my life even when I did not realize it; however, in hindsight I see and now acknowledge God's grace throughout my life experiences. I feel blessed about my decision to go into the military. I signed up on the buddy plan, and although my best friend backed out, I still joined the Air Force. God saw me through basic training and tech school, where I experienced male ignorance, racism, and attempted sexual harassment. He gave me peace of mind during 3 tours to the port mortuary. I was able to endure through the entire experience.

God blessed me to serve in the military for 35 years, through the good and bad, and to negotiate a balance between civilian employment and military employment. There were numerous conflicts, envy and jealousy from co-workers, and resentment from managers at times. I lost promotions and salary increases due to absence from my bank employer. Sometimes I had to say no to military opportunities out of concern for maintaining civilian employment.

I thank God for deployments to Saudi Arabia, Kuwait, Afghanistan, Oman, Greece, and Spain.

Incidents occurred shortly before or after leaving these countries, but I had a safe experience. Also, I thank Him for the opportunity to have boots on the ground, religious programs, services, Bible studies, and counseling. I'm grateful for being an ear, a shoulder to lean on, a sounding board, a solution to a problem, and for directing the Airmen to the Chaplain or the Chaplain to the Airmen.

By faith, I left my job in 2008 for a 6- month deployment and never returned to my position. This was God's grace. I did not like my job, and when my boss called to ask me when I would return to work, without thinking I blurted out that I could not come back to that job. I had not prepared financially and did not know my options or anything, but God provided. I am blessed by my father's influence on my life. He taught me to always save, pay my bills and live frugally.

This lifestyle, and God's Grace, allowed me to retire at age 62. God has allowed me to have so many opportunities to meet people who have touched my life, to go to the places I was able to visit, and to have the sights I have seen over my lifetime. God covered my mistakes and poor choices and continues to cover me! Doing this interview with Constance Cotton has caused me to reflect and acknowledge God's grace in my life daily. Finally, and very, very importantly, God has allowed me good health.[4]

---

[4] Avery Johnson, interviewed by author, Cherry Hill, NJ, March 5, 2016.

KAITLIN MURRAY – Military Sexual Trauma

I met Kaitlin Murray at a Veterans Resource Fair in 2013. She was a vendor addressing military sexual trauma. We are Facebook friends, and both of us post veteran information and resources often. We also attend veteran events together.

What is your military background?

Kaitlin: My name is Kaitlin Murray and I am an active duty Gulf War- era woman veteran who is a survivor of military sexual assault. I transitioned to my home of record upon ending my term of service 22 years ago in Philadelphia, PA, where I enlisted in the Army Reserves and the National Guard. I was honorably discharged, and my final release was in March of 2008. It is my belief that my understanding, experience, and relationship with God caused me to be able to persevere through adversity and help others who share these same experiences. Because I was a single parent, I enlisted in the US Army for economic reasons. I wanted to pursue my education and become an attorney, and to raise my son in a rural environment where I believed we could better achieve our goals and live without many factors which would threaten our ambitions in an urban community.

During my service, I encountered several dilemmas that any woman would be challenged by. After being held hostage on my post by my superiors, I escaped to the Pentagon, where I found refuge. A Pentagon 15-6 (an investigation) ensued. An unorthodox precedent occurred while serving; I did have a victorious outcome to a 15-6 Pentagon investigation, which was "founded;" and to date stands alone to this credit. While serving on active duty, I withstood retaliation, harassment, and other terroristic acts. Subsequently, following my transition from active duty, I was provided the opportunity to present my case to Congress and The Department of Veteran's Affairs Committee on Women's Health. I gave testimony on my experience and contributed to the mandate supported by legislation which required that there be a women's facility in all VA hospitals throughout the United States of America.

How are you helping veterans?

Kaitlin: I continue to advocate and contribute to the senate and congressional legislative bodies at every level of government. This is the foundation for the nonprofit I founded, which became the first functioning organization to address victims of military sexual assault from a grassroots perspective in the United States.

What have been your greatest accomplishments in advocating for veterans- especially women veterans?

Kaitlin: The women veteran's advocacy platform, which has increased and become more aggressive over the past 23 years since I spoke before Congress, continues to unite a population of empowered women of the Armed Forces to address military sexual assault and other gender- specific issues and concerns relating to our military experience.

There have been many milestones which we contributed to the broadened platforms established for addressing women veterans. However, we continue to discover the need to raise the consciousness of many, and to connect with those who have been withdrawn and alienated from these institutions, which have failed us on so many levels. It is evident that the problems are systemic and complex for many reasons, but they create a barrier for getting help and services to deserving women of the armed forces from all eras of war and combat theaters. This unites us, and for some reasons, separates us to date. The greatest accomplishment to note with advocating for veterans – especially women veterans- is the understanding and belief that we have advanced our agendas, which include many levels of knowledgeable and active advocates. This brings about a transparency and congruency that are required to tackle those barriers and factors that present as obstacles and challenges for both women and men veterans. However, it is women who have been silenced by the most common threats while serving in the Armed Forces, and this is where we focus our efforts for the most part today.

What are the main issues you address?

Kaitlin: The multi-tiered and complex issues facing women of the Armed Forces have been discovered in the lives of women who ultimately came forward and shared their experiences in many environments and platforms. Various venues have been provided that have become trusted environments for individuals who have been withdrawn and alienated from the system, or from the institutional platforms for veterans. This has allowed many providers and nonprofits to focus on specific areas of need for service and support for us. For the issues veterans face, we have created a holistic comprehension and application to healing and help for unresolved issues to include spiritual, clinical, medical, psychological, social and other undefined factors and concerns which preclude wholeness and the ability to function.

There are no issues that I, or the community or network of veteran advocates, will not address, once identified, and there are growing needs for service and support groups, organizations, and others to fulfill these needs across the country. Moreover, spirituality creates a foundation for defining specific problems and offering a basis for service and support. There have been successes and proven outcomes of healing personally experienced by men and women veterans, and the creation of "Women Veterans Pray" is a very serious platform for bringing women together who suffer in silence. An environment is offered there for military women who share similar military experiences to share and connect with others.

Has your faith in God and the church helped you?

Kaitlin: The answer specifically for me is "yes," and the reason is best described by my upbringing and spiritual understanding prior to service. As a victim of MST, or military sexual assault, it is imperative that there be some relationship or connection between you and "God" even if religious or other ritualistic affiliations or associations are absent. There are many environments that present potential threats of violence or other offenses which may prove to be a major challenge, and without the presence of God, or belief in a "higher power" or "being," it is more difficult to fulfill the requirements you have contractually agreed to meet in a military function or other obligation. This is especially true when an unfortunate situation occurs that may have lifelong effects, and which stagnates the transition from military experience. The realization may come sooner or later for some, or it may never surface in those whose spirituality is absent, or for whom some prior experience does not exist in the lives of the veteran.

However, for those who have experiences in "church" or other environments where these encounters become learned, veterans ultimately resort to that understanding, and they gain the strength needed to endure and persevere. In some cases, this may not happen soon enough, and alternatively must be re-introduced through offers of suggestion or recommendation, when a Chaplain or minister is sought, to provide the opportunity for intervention or counsel. Finally, it is my experience that in the holistic, psychosocial rehabilitation approach to healing in the lives of veterans who suffer from trauma or other transitioning difficulty, there must be some intervention; it may not always be construed as spiritual, or a connection with "God." However, it is paramount and necessary that an intervention occurs with a knowledgeable professional who is skilled in utilizing specific models in counseling and guiding particular "victims' to be able to function. That professional must understand the multiple and complex factors of each individual as he or she provides help that contributes to the victim's care and recovery.

What do you think is lacking with the care of women veterans?

Kaitlin: For some, the levels of care being offered by military providers within the VA system have been the result of an unquestionably failed methodology. To others, it has had varying levels of success depending on several identifiers, including training, understanding, compassion and other factors. However, I believe that the most important factor "lacking" is that the systemic and fundamental core of the treatment methodology offered reflects the lack of understanding of the culture and environments that these conditions originate in. This understanding is not a part of the fundamentals of the providers' training. The providers' lack of knowledge of the culture that they've committed to care for inhibits their compassion and desire to assist.

At present, there is more input from the actual environment of origin, as opposed to the clinical and medical platforms which contain only a degree of understanding of the traditional psychological and medical ailments supported by the DSM-V. The use of these platforms is considered effective, but it is not in all cases. The military community has become entrenched in the process of training and teaching those who are providers and caregivers, so they can offer a more effective and successful outcome for veterans. I believe that veterans who are educated and empowered, and who actively become involved in their "self-help" treatment, can learn to navigate the many service and support platforms available to them. They will fare better than those who depend totally on the system. How much they are fundamentally in control of the outcomes will be determined by their knowledge of and applicability toward their own healing and ultimate rehabilitation and recovery, particularly from mental and psychological conditions which are present. I believe these agencies provide hope to those who have challenges both now and in the future.

Furthermore, while there is research, clinical trials, and experimentation that may or may not contribute to determining what works, in the meantime the veterans are vulnerable; they experience adverse and far too often irreversible circumstances affecting their health, quality of life and ability to function. It is my belief that we must be realistic about the myths, truths and realities concerning what is happening to human beings; we must take our heads out of the sand and determine who is ultimately responsible for those of us who make the ultimate sacrifice for the freedoms of others in our country and in the world.

So, in conclusion, I would declare to the community of veterans and the clergy, the spiritual community, and ultimately the church, that the need for understanding and compassion is significant, vital, and necessary in the lives of veterans. We must take a moral position to uplift the souls of those who suffer, using compassion and love through our elections in ministry, evangelism, and discipleship, without the interference of conversion or proselytizing. We should fulfill God's commission and charge in Matthew 28:19-20: King James Version (KJV)

(19): "Go ye therefore, and teach all nations, baptizing them in the name of the Father, and of the Son, and of the Holy Ghost, (20) teaching them to observe all things whatsoever I have commanded you: and, lo, I am with you always, even unto the end of the world." Amen.

Finally, we should use that which was prophesized long before the Christ's birth, in Isaiah 61: "The Spirit of the Lord GOD is upon me; because the LORD hath anointed me to preach good tidings unto the meek; he hath sent me to bind up the brokenhearted, to proclaim liberty to the captives, and the opening of the prison to them that are bound; (2) To proclaim the acceptable year of the LORD, and the day of vengeance of our God; to comfort all that mourn; (3) To appoint unto them that mourn in Zion, to give unto them beauty for ashes, the oil of joy for mourning, the garment of praise for the spirit of heaviness; that they might be called trees of righteousness, the planting of the LORD, that he might be glorified."[5]

---

[5] Kaitlin Murray, telephone interview, interviewed by author, March 7, 2016.

SHARON MILLER – Military Sexual Trauma

In 2014, I met Sharon Miller at church, and we have attended classes together at seminary. As we shared our military experiences, she told me about the pain that consumes her as a military sexual trauma victim.

What was your most traumatizing experience in the military?

Sharon: I remember very clearly, as a young soldier in the Army stationed in Germany, that women just were not respected, believed, or valued. On two occasions another soldier, a male who just so happened to be the Captain's Assistant, touched me inappropriately. The second time he did It, I was caught off guard in a stairwell when he grabbed my breasts.

Did anyone in the military help you?

Sharon: I reported this sexual assault through my chain of command, and nothing happened to him. He was to simply stay away from me. I, on the other hand, was shamed and ridiculed by the other soldiers in my unit for months to come. He told them lies about me. I was called names and talked about as if I were to blame, and it made me sick. I walked on eggshells for some time during this period, and I experienced what I now know to be depression; but I got no help or support at all. I didn't know how to seek mental health help, and no one followed up with me. No one helped. I felt alone for a long time, but I didn't think I could do anything about my situation.

How has military sexual trauma changed your life?

Sharon: Things eventually went back to normal, as people stopped talking about me and laughing at me, but I was changed. I knew I couldn't trust authority any longer, and this showed me that the military was no different from the rest of the world. In my eyes, I saw that male soldiers would be protected; female soldiers were not valued and would not be. I never spoke to anyone at the VA when I came home. I should have, but I decided to put it all behind me. I saw a lot of sexual impropriety in Basic Training, at AIT, and on my permanent duty assignment, and nothing was ever done to the male military members who were getting girls pregnant at Basic and AIT; they were simply transferred, while the girl was forced to leave the Army. It was crazy, so I guess it shouldn't have surprised me when nothing was done in my case.

The men took advantage of us because they could. They knew they were safe from prosecution. I had a Drill Sergeant take advantage of me as well. There was no intercourse, but there were sexual advances. We had no voice. I was only 20. Needless to say, when I left the regular Army and entered the reserves, I was on guard for this type of behavior, but it was still prevalent.

Has your church helped you with MST?

Sharon: I have never spoken about my experiences of sexual abuse in the army with anyone at church, although I experienced abuse as a child and have spoken about those things. I have been saved all my life, and I am sure that my faith is what held me up during those times and kept me from quitting. However, this experience left a deep scar. I was young, scared and alone. Just writing about it makes me sick to my stomach, and I feel it all over again. Women should not have to go through things like this.[6]

---

[6] Sharon Miller, interviewed by author, Philadelphia, PA, March 8, 2016.

LINDA SMITH – Post Traumatic Stress Disorder /Military Sexual Trauma

I met Linda Smith in 2015 at a women's veteran retreat. We meet at women veteran events and occasionally talk on the phone.

How long were you in the military and what were your duty assignments?

Linda: I am a Black female, 60 years old, from Camden, NJ. I spent 10 years in the Army as an enlisted soldier for about 18 months, and the remainder of my time as a Commissioned Officer. I resigned from active duty in 1989. I did not resign my Commission; I was told I would have to go through Congress to do so. I'm not really sure if that is true.

Did any of your family members serve in the military?

Linda: I am a Cold War Veteran who served after the Vietnam War and before Desert Storm. I come from a family of veterans, with family members serving during every war the United States participated in since WWI, and possibly prior to that; we are still tracing our family history. My grandfather served during WWI, and my father and all 5 of my mother's brothers served during WWII. I saw an old Camden newspaper article where my maternal grandmother received an award as a "5 Star Mother" for having 5 sons in WWII at the same time. My mother also had a female cousin who served in WWII. My younger brother served during Desert Storm, my brother-in-law during the Korean War, and my nephew served in both

Iraq and Afghanistan. Also, an assortment of cousins, both male and female, have served, and some are still on active duty. Most of them used their military and veteran benefits to increase social, educational, and economic opportunities for themselves and their family members.

When and why did you join the military?

Linda: I was about 25 when I joined the army in 1979. I graduated from Douglass College, Rutgers University, in New Brunswick, in 1977, and majored in sociology. I dreamed of righting all social problems and started my quest by working for the Urban League in New Brunswick for about 2 years. I enjoyed my work and considered myself a "community and social activist." I had no intention of following the family tradition of military service. However, I originally ran away from home just to attend college in New Brunswick; my Father wanted me to attend Rutgers in Camden as a commuter, since it was his belief a proper young lady does not leave the home until she is married! But I had a bad case of wanderlust; I was an avid reader since age 5 and wanted to see other places and meet other people like in the books I read. I also was interested in why people were so different.

After a while, I wanted to see more than NY, Philly and NJ, so I met a very nice- looking guy who heard me talking about my desire to travel the world, and he offered to assist me with accomplishing my dreams. I thought he was interested in me as a potential girlfriend, but he turned out to be an Army Recruiter, so I joined the Army! There were many other reasons that led to my joining as well, such as the education benefits for graduate school. I didn't tell any of my friends or my so- called social activist colleagues that I enlisted in the army.

Overall, I found the army to be a welcome challenge! Since I was raised in a well-disciplined home, I could go with the flow. I was amazed by my physical transformation, and I welcomed it. I came to love running and the overall healthy appearance that resulted from the physical training required by the Army. Unlike a lot of women who joined the Army prior to the mid-70's, I did not receive Basic Training at Ft. McClellan, Ft. Jackson, or in the all-female units, but was sent to a "one station unit training" at Ft. Gordon, GA, for both basic and AIT, in a unit with predominately male recruits. I shared the same barracks, which was, to my understanding, a new concept for the Army.

What were your duty assignments in the military?

Linda: After successful completion of Basic and AIT, I was assigned to Ft. Hood, TX, as a Radio Operator in the 2nd Armored Division Artillery. I was one of about 5 women in a Company of approximately 200 men! It was so weird when I first arrived on the back of the "deuce and a half." The men acted as though they had never seen a woman before! When entering Basic Training, the Drill Sergeants hollered and screamed at us to lift and carry our heavy bags off the trucks, which I felt I needed help with, but then the men were breaking their necks to help me carry my bags off the truck. I was annoyed and shocked at their demands to help me. Also, not only were there few women in my Company, but we were surrounded by Infantry,

Armor and other Artillery Brigades, so there were few women in the entire area!

Even though I grew up with primarily male relatives, I never saw so many men in my life. I got along with the guys great! I was friendly with everyone regardless of whether they were white, black, or brown (and no, I was not promiscuous, as was the stereotype for female soldiers at that time). I worked in the S3 as the Radio Operator for the Colonel, so to speak, and became familiar with the Field Grade Officers at the command and staff level. About a year into my unit, the S3 talked to me about Officer Candidate School (OCS). I had already been accepted into flight school, but the Colonel urged me to look into OCS; before I knew it, the Division Commander signed off on my application packet and I was off to OCS! I also went to parachute training and earned my airborne patch. I considered myself a "lean, green fighting machine"! I was among the top young Officers at my first post, Ft. McClellan, AL, but there was a secret I was hiding that 10 years later lead to my decline. I was sexually assaulted by the Chaplain, who was also a Captain, two weeks prior to my leaving for OCS.

Was it difficult to for you to adjust to civilian life?

Linda: After I resigned from the Army in May of 1989, it was very difficult to adjust to civilian life. I felt alone and alienated, as if I had settled in another country with different values. It was truly a cultural shock! I didn't stay in contact with my friends in the military, and it was difficult making new friends. I decided to stay in New Orleans instead of returning home to NJ. I found employment in law enforcement jobs and was able to attend the University of New Orleans graduate program majoring in sociology. I had a 4.0 average during my first 3 semesters.

To make a very long story short, for many years I did not know I was a veteran. Although many of my family members were veterans, I thought one had to be in a war to be one. I had many challenges after leaving the military. I lost all my furniture and personal property that I had left in military storage, because I was not able to afford a house large enough for them. While in graduate school, my father lost his long struggle with cancer and died. Exactly a year later my mother, who was together with my father for 60 years, was very despondent after my father's death and went missing in NJ while I was living in New Orleans. Her body was found after the snow cleared. I wanted to die even more myself. However, after an unsuccessful attempt at suicide while I was in the army, I resorted to living a somewhat risky lifestyle in hopes of dying. Later, as I was gradually getting my life together, Hurricane Katrina struck. I lived in New Orleans East, which was severely hit by the initial storm surge.

Many people in other areas were affected by the levees bursting. I was not part of the group at the convention center or the Saint's stadium. The hurricane was devastating; not because of the destruction of the storm itself, but because of the way people reacted. I felt I witnessed the worst of human nature. It was unbelievable! I was finally evacuated to South Carolina and sent to a veterans hospital for care. I was evaluated there, and that's when it was discovered that I was a survivor of military sexually assault. I did not feel comfortable talking about it, much less filing a claim for compensation. Eventually I was provided a plane ticket home after a TV interview on FOX news. It was during my time in South Carolina that I also saw the best of human nature. Skipping over a few years, I became homeless in 2009.

I have a family member who is a drug and alcohol counselor at the Philadelphia VA Hospital, and she told me about the HUDVASH program. The office was on the 8th floor of the hospital. It was very difficult getting assistance because I was a single female with no children, and therefore was told I was low in priority for receiving assistance. After so many years of wanting to die, I learned from Hurricane Katrina that I wanted to live. Since I struggled for my life, I also had the courage to assist others in their survival, so I wasn't taking "no" for an answer. I learned a lot from talking to other veterans and followed up by reading as much as I could on veteran's support and services, as well as benefits. I also followed up on a claim for PTSD/MST. I found it even more difficult to get assistance with my claim for MST.

I was made to feel shame and was told I was arrogant by many Service organizations for filing a PTSD/MST claim. After a big controversy, I did get the HUDVASH voucher. I met many male veterans (but very few females) who provided me with information on where to find assistance. I was told to seek help at the Veterans Multi-Service Center in Philadelphia. It was difficult to find because most veterans called it" The Perimeter" or" The Bridge," so I was confused.

Anyway, I found it. I was able to get assistance with my claim, which I started in 2009. Because of the VMC's help, I eventually received 70% in 2011 and 100% in 2014. It wasn't until about 2013 that I saw an article in the newspaper about the Women's Veteran Center at the VMC. It was just opening (whatever year that was). I went down there and met the founder, and noticed we had many things in common. I became a regular, and soon volunteered. It was a great feeling meeting other women veterans and re-establishing that feeling of comradery I shared with my long- lost military friends. Social events were a great way to network with the women; we shared life experiences and acquired and exchanged much- needed information.

The many health and fitness workshops are a reminder we must continue to strive for healthy living. There are various other workshops in other areas, such as entrepreneurship and developing skills for a successful employment search. The various "retreats" are very helpful in learning relaxation techniques useful in managing stress and anxiety. The services support, my experiences with the Veteran Medical Center (VMC), and especially the Women Veteran Center (WVC), together with the support at VA Hospital, have directly contributed to my commitment to living a healthy lifestyle. I went from being homeless to owning my own home and going back to school at my alma mater, Rutgers University, to finish graduate school. I feel obliged to share my experiences- the ups and downs- to encourage other women veterans that you are never so far down that you can't get back up and accomplish your goals.

Did you experience prejudice, discrimination, or racism in the military?

Linda: Prejudice, discrimination, and racism appear to be facts of life. Therefore, although social change is necessary and continuous, my parents and extended family valued striving to be the best at whatever you do to be successful, no matter the circumstances. If one is a street cleaner, then be the best street cleaner you can be, even if you have to work twice as hard as anyone else. Even though my parents were keenly aware of the negative effects of prejudice, discrimination, and racism, this was no excuse for failure. So being both female and Black and living in America, one would certainly experience these ills anywhere and almost everywhere at varying degrees. The army is no different. Two incidents in the army regarding gender and race impacted my life in a major way. When I was an enlisted soldier, I was sexually assaulted by the Chaplain two weeks prior to leaving to attend the Officer Candidate School, (OCS) at Ft. Benning, GA. I immediately reported it to my chain of command. The First Sergeant refused to address the "incident" because he told me he no longer considered me an enlisted soldier, since I had been accepted to OCS.

The incident was handed over to the Company Commander to address. Basically, my Commander informed me that if I pressed charges against the Chaplain, I would never receive my Commission, since officers must stick together. I, of course went on to attend OCS. That decision has haunted me to this day on many levels. The second incident related to race occurred with the new First Sergeant, who came to our company shortly before I was accepted to both flight school and OCS. He felt that as a Black person I was acting "too big for my britches." I also attended graduate school in the evening, which he tried to prevent, but the Sergeant overruled him. The First Sergeant would often catch me alone and berate me for going to school, since he "didn't know any niggers with degrees," which I knew was nonsense. After the harassment came too often, I reported it to the Equal Opportunity NCO; however, the EO NCO, who was also Black, asked me not to pursue a racial discrimination report against the First Sergeant.

He consulted with the unit senior NCO's, and they felt it would bring negative consequences for me, since the First Sergeant was well-connected. I discovered this was not altogether true; it spoke to the fears of that particular NCO and some of the other NCO's, just as the incident with the Chaplain was more related to fears of the Commander and some of the other Officers. They had no concern about me; they were only concerned for their own careers and did not wish to "ruffle any feathers." Had I pursued both incidents, it would have likely had a negative impact on the careers of a few people, and that was the concern.

The negative part about it was not what happened to me, but the failure of the Command to address the offenses. They only wanted to prevent a "scandal," to not draw attention to a controversial incident that's best kept undercover. In retrospect, I came to realize it was more complicated than that; it involved issues of both race and gender in a larger context. I was fortunate, in many ways, that because of my upbringing, I was able to some extent put these incidents behind me. I had a successful career in my 10 years; however, the incidents also left scars that affect me now and will for the rest of my life.

How has God and your faith helped you?

Linda: I've had a relationship with God since childhood and was raised in the church. My faith has grown a lot, and I trust God with my life. Some days I'm not comfortable leaving my house, but God is healing and helping me with my fears.[7]

---

[7] Linda Smith, interviewed by author, Camden, NJ, March 13, 2016.

SHERRI MILES

In 2016, I met Sherri Miles when we were introduced to one another by a VA nurse. Sherri wrote a book about her military experience. We talk on the phone occasionally.

What branch of the military were you in and how long?

Sherri: I was in the Army for 6 active duty years and in the Army Reserves for 7 years.

What were your military occupations and duties?

Sherri: On active duty I was a Radio Operator, which I loved doing. I worked in Korea with I Corps Communication Company. Our team worked for the Sergeant Major, so we only went out on missions if he went out. I worked in the Mars Station, where I patched calls by radio between soldiers overseas and their families. I totally loved it! I also had the opportunity to work alongside an air traffic control company. We were 3 female Radio Operators who monitored and controlled all the radio air traffic in our area, which was Jui Jong Bu, Korea. We were sure we were the only all- female African American team of Radio Operators. It was 1978, and female Radio Operators were rare back then. It was a combat position, but women were not yet allowed to go into combat.

I chose Radio Operator over a clerical position because I wanted to do something different. I went in the military because I wanted to be adventurous. Prior to the military all I did was work for low wages, party, smoke weed, and snort methamphetamines. To me it seemed my life was spiraling out of control. It was peacetime in America after the Vietnam era, so at age 23 I joined the Army. And I chose the Army over the Air Force because I felt it would challenge me. It did. I grew up while in the military; what I mean is I matured while in the military. I also worked in a signal company for a while, and Military Intelligence in an Army Security Agency at Ft. Polk, Louisiana.

What were some of the challenges and blessings you experienced in the military and as a veteran?

Sherri: I met my husband of 36 years in Jui Jong Bu, Korea. When we both transferred back to the United States, we got married while at Ft. Polk, LA; Ft. Polk is also where I faced my greatest challenge, which has left its print in my heart and my life. Because we were some of the first women to serve beside men, we were mistreated with verbal assaults. Men were hanging out of windows screaming to harm us and stalk us. We were called lesbians and whores. Some were raped; even from their formations they were allowed such. There was no EO yet, no protections set up yet. Some of the Officers in charge were the worst abusers. We learned to travel in groups. We expected that the man in the foxhole had our back, not that he might rape us! The other overseas assignment I did was in Hanau, Germany. I was promoted to Sergeant while there. We lived in Babenhausen, where my husband worked, and I took the train to my Unit. We loved Germany and its culture, but there is nowhere in the world like the United States! We also served at Ft. Benning, in GA, where I was the Assistant Communications Chief.

How has your faith and God helped you?

Sherri: My faith has helped to make me stronger. I still have some issues stemming from the treatment at Ft. Polk, but I try to deal with life one day at a time. Before and when I was in the military, I wasn't saved. I wasn't a Christian. I hadn't accepted Christ. I knew Him; I was raised in the church, but I did not profess him until my early 40's. I realize now that God was always there protecting me, and He was blessing me even when I wasn't serving Him. He allowed me to live long enough to serve Him. I thank Him so much. He is my anchor, my Superior Officer, my Squad Leader, and my Drill Sergeant. Having faith in him and being obedient to the word of God both help me deal with life's issues with hope instead of dread, courage instead of fear, and love for others to see beyond the hard hearts of some. At the same time, I am a warrior; a Prayer Warrior![8]

---

[8] Sherri Miles, interviewed by author, Sicklerville, NJ, March 15, 2016.

MAY BRILL

I met May Brill at "Operation: I AM Women: A Women Veterans Symposium." She inspired me by her enthusiasm to teach people about the history of women in the military.

When and where did you serve in the military and what were your duties?

May: During World War II I joined the Women Accepted for Volunteer Emergency Service (WAVES). I was in WAVES for two years, in the Supply Corps for the Pacific Fleet and Pacific bases. I was stationed in Oakland, CA, but I was from Philadelphia. Women were sent to Hunter College for Women for training.

What challenges did you face in the military?

May: I was a female and I was Jewish; we were the only Jewish girls out of 400 people. They did not know what a Jewish person was like because they didn't know any Jewish people their whole lives. The training was the same as the men.

As a veteran, what do you see as challenges for women veterans?

May: As a person from a poor family, I had no idea I could go to college. After I came home from the military, I went to Temple University. Because of my two years in the military, I was entitled to two years of college. After I married and had four children, my husband said that I should go back to school, and I graduated from Camden County Community College, then went to Glassboro College, where they taught me gerontology. I got a job as an assistant manager at an apartment complex. We took care of 500 seniors living there. No one knew how to take care of older people except me. My education in gerontology taught me how to help people live longer. I am concerned about women veterans committing suicide.

What are you currently doing for women veterans?

May: At 94 years old, I am Chairman of Women in the Military for the State of New Jersey. I speak to women about past military situations that women faced, and I encourage women to serve proudly. I tell them they should be proud to be a woman.

How has God and your faith helped you?

May: I believe that God has watched over me and my life and made my course in life to do my best for women in the military and veterans. I believe that I'm still here because I have answered the call on my life that God has placed in me to take care of women who served in the military. God has blessed me to have 11 grandchildren and several great grandchildren.

Did your family members serve in the military?

May: My husband was in the Navy for 3 1/2 years during World War II, and he raised our children to be proud of women, because women can be anything they want to be if they try. I am Senior Vice Commander of Jewish VFW Post 126 and we do for the troops. We do for the veterans, and we are there to spread the word that veterans are important. I go to organizations and speak about women and the history of women in the military. Women had to wear men's clothes at the beginning in the military. Molly Pitcher fought in the revolutionary war when her husband collapsed, and she took over for him in men's clothes. She influenced women to have women's clothes. I was there when women wore military uniforms for the first time. Only the nuns and people who were helping us soldiers were in women's clothes at that time. It has been only three years ago that women could get a lawyer for sexual abuse or sexual harassment incidents in the military. When you were in the military, you could be sexually harassed or discriminated against because of your religion or color. In 1949, WAVES and WACS were considered a part of the Army, Navy, Air Force, and Marines.[9]

---

[9] May Brill, interviewed by author, Blackwood, NJ, March 26, 2016.

May Brill has inspired and supported many women veterans, including our friend Selina Kanowitz, who was installed as the first female Commander of the Jewish War Veterans Post 126 in June 2017. Commander Kanowitz was awarded Post Commander of the Year for 2017-2018 at the state and national levels. Commander Kanowitz served in the U.S. Air Force Reserves and worked as a Radiologic Technologist for over 21 years before retirement. She held the rank of Master Sergeant when she retired.

May, Selina, Julia, Selina's friend, and I participated in a video entitled "Jewish War Veterans "Women in Military Life". Our video can be found on YouTube. In the video, we discuss issues related to women in the military from World War II to the present.

MILITARY FAMILIES

I am not sure I fully considered that my choice to serve my country would also have such a profound effect on my family, but it did not take long to come to that realization.

Military families also serve their country. They often experience separation from their military loved ones who are deployed and required to be away from home for various duty assignments. Military families also endure issues like abandonment, infidelity, readjustment, and abuse. Unfortunately, they must cope with grief in many ways. This can be in the form of death, loss of military status and benefits, or of dealing with the medical and mental challenges of the servicemember. Family members and friends may feel that their "own sense of peace and happiness is greatly compromised. As family and friends, we want desperately to help and support the warrior. We want to heal and love them, but oftentimes we feel alone and helpless in the battle. We may be well- aware of the high price the warrior has paid for our freedom and the freedom of others. Now, we, too, pay a price for that service."[10]

As women and men serve around the world, they still desire to have families like their civilian counterparts, and:

> There are an increasing number of women in the military, and dual military couples that are serving in developing areas of conflict around the world. Many of these women are mothers, and many of their children are very young. While many of these children are cared for by members of their extended family, and do receive lots of love and attention, the full extent of how much the lack of attachment to the child's

---

[10] Edward Tick. *War and the Soul: Healing Our Nation's Veterans from Post-traumatic Stress Disorder.* (Illinois: Theosophical Publishing House, 2005), 102.

own mother will impact development later in life is not fully known.[11]

From 2012 to present, I have witnessed and been affected emotionally by the hardships and challenges of having a female war veteran in my family. I have changed my family members' names for confidentiality. My niece, Trina White, served in the military for 6 years before her enlistment expired. During her time in the military she was a cook and was stationed in Texas and Germany. Trina also served two tours in the Iraq War. While in Germany, she married and had a son. At her last duty assignment in Iraq, Trina joined a church led by a pastor who also worked as a civilian contractor. She joined the choir and became very involved in church activities during the war.

---

[11] Schneider, Eugene William III. "Practical Pastoral Care: Observations from a Military Chaplain in Dealing with Trauma" (PhD diss., Lutheran Theological Seminary Philadelphia, 2009), 13.

My sister, Marge Miller, was the caregiver for Trina's son Lee. My sister has some medical problems but was willing to care for her grandson again like she had done the first time my niece went to Iraq because she wanted him to be well cared- for, and they had a close bond.

When Trina came home from Iraq, she was distraught and full of anxiety. She stayed in Germany and my sister took her son to her. The tours of war took a toll on her family and she divorced her husband, which made her a single mother. Trina left the military and told my sister that she was moving to Atlanta because the pastor in Iraq was starting a church there, and most of the soldiers who fellowshipped together in Iraq were also moving there to become members of the new church. Trina wanted to raise Lee as a single mom, and she tried her best. Unfortunately, she was diagnosed with thyroid cancer and PTSD. She became cancer-free after a year, but her PTSD became worse. Trina asked my sister to adopt Lee and she did. He moved to South Carolina with his grandmother, where he still resides.

For the last four years, Marge and Trina's relationship has been rocky. Lee's father remarried, and he is still full- time in the Army. He went to Iraq a few years ago. Sadly, he makes promises to Lee that he doesn't keep, and Trina does the same. Both parents rarely visit Lee, and he struggles with the idea that his parents don't want him. My sister works hard caring for him, but her health has deteriorated. Over the years I have been very concerned about my sister and niece. Trina's and my relationship have been estranged at times. Trina told me that from the time she was about 13 years old, she wanted to go into the Army like me.

We have shared some special times together, especially when she came to stay with me when I was stationed in Augusta, GA. She helped me care for my oldest son while I worked when he was an infant. Trina and I were in the military at the same time for a few years, and we communicated often. After she came back from war our relationship changed, but I helped her apply for her VA benefits, and supported her when she wanted to talk. We prayed and read scriptures together.

In January 2014, my sister and I planned a sisters' getaway weekend in Charlotte, NC. The idea was mine, because every time I talked to her a few months prior, she would tell me how stressed out she was about raising Lee and dealing with Trina. Alex was having abandonment issues, demonstrating destructive behavior, and showing anger. Marge was medically retired around that time; she had been a judge. Trina was having mental breakdowns and shared that she was sexually assaulted in Iraq. When she would visit my sister's house, she would have crying spells and tantrums, and she would talk about being a bad mother to Lee.

My sister needed a break. I flew to Charlotte, NC. I thought Marge needed time away from her home, so she picked me up from the airport and we stayed at a hotel about an hour from her house. We had so much fun going out to eat, visiting a museum, shopping, and going to a comedy club. I also needed to get away, as I was coping with teenage sons, health challenges, and stress from various parts of my life. I cherish the time we spent together, especially since she is my best friend. I interviewed her in order to reveal the difficulties military families endure.

THE MILITARY FAMILY STORY CONTINUES – THE CONVERSATION

When did your daughter Trina go to war?
Marge: My daughter Trina was deployed in December of 2002 the first time, and in April of 2004 the second time.

Did you care for your daughter Trina's son? If so, why were you selected?

Marge: Yes, I did care for my grandson. I was selected because even though my daughter was married, her husband was not equipped to handle a five-month-old child because he was also in the military and had to prepare to go to war also.

What challenges occurred while caring for your grandson?

Marge: In 2002 I had school age children, one entering high school and another who has learning disabilities. I had a job and a husband, and I was also attending college, taking classes to earn my degree, and working a part-time job. Taking on another responsibility was both physically and mentally challenging. It affected my social life. The family dynamics changed. It appeared to me that the structured routine I had going fell to the wayside, and I was on autopilot, jumping from one task to the next without much forethought. I was exhausted most of the time and felt isolated handling the demands of my new life.

When Trina came home, did you notice any changes with her?

Marge: When my daughter came home the first time, she came to get her son and returned to Germany- no questions asked. I wanted her to start her life and I felt it was not too late for her to bond with her son and husband. I wished her well. It was a short- lived reunion; she was redeployed 6 months later. A lot was going on with her, but she did not tell us. It was as if she was no longer my child. Her mentality was a sovereign entity; she belonged to no one here. When she returned the second time, her son was 5. The woman who came to get him was a stranger. She didn't come home; she came to get her son, and she moved to another state with the soldiers she bonded with while deployed. She didn't even tell us her plans until closer to her return. She came, and two days later she was gone.

Did Trina bond with her son upon returning from war?

Marge: They bonded in sorts, but not as mother and son. When she took him to Atlanta, I told her not to discipline him right away; just love him and be patient with him, because he had to know she was his caregiver before disciplinary measures could be enacted. I remember the two of them would call on separate phones, telling on each other. She would be calling for her mother's advice and he would be calling for his mother's help. It was emotional because I wanted her to have her child, but clearly she was not the mother. He was five and running away from home. He left the house in footed pajamas and his coat; luckily no harm came to him.

Did Trina take her son Lee to live with her?

Marge: Several times, but it wouldn't work out.

Was Trina capable or willing to care for Lee?

Marge: I think she loved him, but she wasn't capable of caring for him. She had difficulty just getting him to school on a regular basis. She tried to provide for him but being structured was hard for her. She was fun but absent most of the time. He suffered from a detachment disorder that required years of therapy.

How has Trina's life in the military affected your family?

Marge: It is still affecting my family. My husband and I are still raising our grandson.

We finished raising our children and should be empty nesters, but we are just getting him to high school. The fallout of adopting our grandchild is continuous as he gets older, and he raises more questions. It has become apparent that his parents, for whatever reason at the time, did not do the right thing for him.

Did Trina have medical issues after the war?

Marge: Yes; she was affected by cancer, PTSD, carpal tunnel, vision loss, and depression. Lee, according to his doctors, suffers from PTSD, reactive detachment disorder, anxiety, aggressive response to anger, and Attention Deficit Disorder (ADD).

How has being Lee's caregiver impacted you?

Marge: Some days I feel good about my decision and I know it was the right one, but most days I feel deprived of my life. It is not because of raising my grandson, but because I see his parents living their life, traveling, socializing, or doing whatever they want to do. They are enjoying their lives, and as I remember that they didn't make Lee their priority, it makes me angry. I think my health issues are due to the stress and anxiety I feel.

How has God, your faith, or the church helped you?

Marge: I know God was there every step of the way. People ask how I did it all these years, and I know it was by God's grace. I'm able to forgive every one of their shortcomings and do what is best for my grandson, and that also means including his parents in his life. I'm able to move forward, and I know in the end all will be well with Lee and with the relationship he has with his parents. I have faith that God is healing all of us, and that I am here for this purpose. It's no big deal for grandparents to raise their grandchildren nowadays. I think my church is supportive of me and my family. However, I wish they had programs to assist military personnel and their families. They pray for us, but it is difficult to raise Lee sometimes; I do it because I love him, and he needs me. I was fortunate I had people to talk it over with, but there are many who have no one but God. Somehow it is enough.

What did the church do to help your family?

Marge: I think my church has done what they could. They have evolved with us. My grandson has a male mentor at church.

Would you do it again?

Marge: When my daughter came to me and told me she was being deployed, I wish I would have advised her to get out. I was so proud when she said she took an oath to serve and protect her country and then signed up. But if I had to do it again, I would have said no, because I would rather not see my daughter with so many medical and mental problems. I would rather have my grandson be with his parents.[12]

After interviewing my sister, I saw the need to tell women veterans' stories because they needed the opportunity to share how their military service affected their lives and relationships. My husband and two sons have shared with me the

---

[12] Marge Stevenson, telephone interview, interviewed by author, March 1, 2016.

challenges they endured living with me. From their stories I have come to realize that:

"When living with a vet who is profoundly affected with PTSD, there can be little doubt that his behavior will in some manner affect those around him. After a while, a family member can develop some of the characteristics of the trauma victim. They, too, may become anxious, overly sensitive, worried, and apprehensive of going out or being around others. They, too, may have problems with concentration and attention. Many nights they may not be able to fall asleep or wake up exhausted."[13]

---

[13] Edward Tick. *War and the Soul: Healing Our Nation's Veterans from Post-traumatic Stress Disorder*. (Illinois: Theosophical Publishing House, 2005), 102.

BACK TO THE VETERANS ADMINISTRATION

The VA was created to provide care and benefits to eligible veterans and their families. The VA has both a good and bad reputation concerning accomplishing its charge and has been in the media often about corruption and mistreatment of veterans. The mission of the VA, according to the Veterans Administration's website, is stated like this: The Department of Veterans Affairs (VA):

"...was established as an independent agency under the President by Executive Order 5398 on July 21, 1930. It was elevated to Cabinet level on March 15, 1989 (Public Law No. 100-527). The VA's mission is to serve America's Veterans and their families with dignity and compassion, and to be their principal advocate in ensuring that they receive medical care, benefits, social support, and lasting memorials promoting the health, welfare, and dignity of all Veterans in recognition of their service to this Nation."[14]

The VA is a huge organization that has:

> ...a central office, which is located in Washington, DC, and field facilities throughout the Nation administered by its three major line organizations: Veterans Health Administration, Veterans Benefits Administration, and National Cemetery Administration. Services and benefits are provided through a nationwide network of 153 hospitals, 784 community-based outpatient clinics, 134 community living centers, 90 domiciliary residential rehabilitation treatment programs, 264 Vet Centers, 57 Veterans benefits regional offices, and 131 national cemeteries.[15]

Veterans must apply for benefits to get housing, education, life insurance, and other entitlements. For medical benefits, "veterans must have a service- connected disability, which means that veterans who are disabled by an

---

[14] http//www.va.org. (accessed March 23, 2016.
[15] Ibid.

injury or illness that was incurred or aggravated during active military service should qualify if their medical records show documentation."[16] Additionally, "VA benefits vary depending on the veteran's service record. A veteran, his/her spouse, and dependents may be eligible for different types of benefits provided by VA."[17]

For war veterans and military sexual trauma veterans, this is the help that is at a Vet Center; it is:

> ... a type of VA health care facility designed to provide outreach and readjustment counseling services through 232 community-based Vet Centers located in all 50 states and the District of Columbia, Guam, Puerto Rico, American Samoa, and the U.S. Virgin Islands. Veterans are eligible if they served on active duty in a combat theater during World War II, the Korean War, the Vietnam War, the Gulf War, or the campaigns in Lebanon, Grenada, Panama,

---

[16] Ibid.
[17] Ibid.

> Somalia, Bosnia, Kosovo, Afghanistan, Iraq, and the Global War on Terror. Veterans who served in the active military during the Vietnam-era, but not in the Republic of Vietnam, must have requested services at a Vet Center before January 1, 2004. Vet Centers do not require enrollment in the VHA Health Care System.[18]

The statistics for veterans clearly show that the VA does not meet the needs of some veterans, partly because they are denied benefits and can wait a long time to be approved for benefits. Other veterans don't want any affiliation with the government. Veterans are suffering and need help from numerous sources.

Over the years I have talked to many veterans of wars who are suffering, but in particular, I want to focus on the suffering of veterans from the Gulf War, Iraq, and Afghanistan wars. There are documentaries on DVD's, titled "Killing Our

---

[18] Ibid.

Own" and "Beyond Treason," which tell the stories of Gulf War veterans who are suffering due to their exposure to toxins and other contaminants. They also give detailed information about the medical problems the soldiers endured during and after the war. Gulf War veterans have high incidences of Lou Gehrig's Disease, also known as Amyotrophic Lateral Sclerosis (ALS). My niece Trina served two tours in Iraq, and shortly after she came home, she was diagnosed with thyroid cancer. Recently she told me that five of the seven women whom she lived with also developed some form of cancer. Vice President Joe Biden's son Beau Biden died from brain cancer after he served in Iraq. There have been countless war veterans who have been diagnosed or died from cancers, as well as mysterious and known medical conditions and illnesses.

Veterans and their families endure a lot of grieving circumstances that stem from military trauma and serving in a war. The reality is:

> ...traumatic events may come while serving our country as a member of the Armed Forces during a time of combat. The list of things that can impact us to induce a traumatic event is almost limitless. Compounding the equation is that what may seem like a traumatic event for one person is seen to be of little cause of concern for another. Such setbacks leave an indelible mark. They color how persons respond to the events that confront and impact life on a daily basis. The memories that are attached to these types of events hold a powerful grip on the internal self. The events are seared into memory. These events bring along much baggage that needs to be processed in order to "move on" with life. While knowing and acknowledging that these situations exist and have an impact on multiple levels (emotionally, physically, spiritually, relationally, to name a few), persons often are reluctant to seek the help that will enable them to deal, to cope,

and to live with the impact of these events. Getting help enables a person to cope.[19]

Many veterans find it hard to cope in society, and that could be the reason that veteran statistics are alarming and grim. Unfortunately, most women veteran statistics are not separate. Even though the VA is available, many veterans are suffering due to the lack of care, denial of benefits, and the problems associated with assimilating back into society. Veterans, especially women, need more assistance from supportive communities like faith organizations to help them transition as a civilian.

THE SUICIDE STATISTICS FOR VETERANS:

> Forty-nine thousand Vietnam War veterans committed suicide between 2005 and 2011. Among recent returnees, reports about their suicides come from every corner of

---

[19] Schneider, Eugene William III. "Practical Pastoral Care: Observations from a Military Chaplain in Dealing with Trauma" (PhD diss., LTSP, 2009), 1.

the United States, as well as from other countries with troops in combat in Iraq and Afghanistan. In Iraq alone, one in five noncombat deaths were due to suicide. Now, Army suicide rates set records as the highest ever. In 2006, almost one-third of the ninety-nine suicides occurred in Iraq and Afghanistan. Failed relationships, legal and financial troubles, work stress, and deployment time all contributed. By May of 2007, 107 troops had committed suicide while in the country. The magnitude of the problem prompted the Army to begin records of suicide attempts for the first time. There were almost 1000 in 2006. In these modern wars, many more veterans die from suicide after they are at war than were killed in combat. Troop suicide is now more lethal than combat.[20]

VIOLENT CRIME STATISTICS:

Many veterans die in violent ways after violent service. Accidents ("unconscious suicides") and criminal activity ("death by cop") may have military or combat-generated components. Iraq and Afghanistan veterans have a 75 percent

---

[20] Edward Tick. *War and the Soul: Healing Our Nation's Veterans from Post-traumatic Stress Disorder.* (Illinois: Theosophical Publishing House, 2005), 40.

higher rate of fatal motor vehicle accidents than non-vets. They are more at risk in the months following deployment, and those serving multiple tours are at the highest risk. "Accidental deaths" may mean that the terrible veteran suicide rate is even higher than we know. Nobody can be sure how many of these incidents are "accidents".[21]

HIGH INCARCERATION STATISTICS:

As of 1998, according to the Department of Justice, out of a national veteran population of over 25 million, 225,000 veterans were held in federal and state prisons. About 56,500 were Vietnam War-era veterans, and 18,500 were Persian Gulf War-era vets. Of those, 20 percent reported serving combat duty and 16 percent were dishonorably discharged. Among other findings: veterans were more likely than non-vets to be in prison for a violent offense; alcohol was more likely to be involved in veteran crimes; while the number of veteran in the United States were declining, the number in prisons was rising; sex offenders constituted one-third of the prisoners held in military correctional facilities; veterans had less-extensive previous criminal records and were more likely to report mental illnesses than civilians. By 2004 the Department of

---

[21] Ibid, 41.

Justice found that 57 percent of imprisoned veterans were incarcerated for a violent offense, a rate 10 percent higher than nonveterans. More recent Department of Justice facts estimate 223,000 veterans in prison, most from the Vietnam War era.[22]

CHILD ABUSE STATISTICS AS A RESULT OF WAR DEPLOYMENTS:

Deployment may increase the rate of child abuse. One study found that rates of child abuse at a Texas military base doubled soon after deployment began. Another found that having a spouse in a combat zone vastly increased the rate of maltreatment of children. The majority of abuse and neglect were perpetrated by the civilian spouse left behind, demonstrating the degree of stress that partners live with, and the ripple effect it has through families.[23]

THE DRUG AND ALCOHOL STATISTICS:

The Substance Abuse and Mental Health Services Administration reported in 2003 that on a monthly basis more veterans used marijuana, were heavy alcohol users, and received more treatment for substance abuse than comparable nonveterans. Additionally, general alcohol use, driving

---

[22] Ibid, 42.
[23] Ibid, 46.

while intoxicated, and smoking were all significantly higher among veterans. The US government estimated that in 2002 and 2003 two million veterans, 8 percent of all veterans, abused alcohol or illicit drugs. Army research found that alcohol misuse rose from 13 percent to 21 percent among soldiers one year after returning from Iraq and Afghanistan. Countless troops testify that they were given many drugs downrange to cope with combat zone difficulties—to go to sleep, to wake up, to get psyched for high-intensity combat, to not feel pain, to forget acts they judge to be wrong. They returned home dependent or addicted.[24]

THE STATISTICS FOR HIGH HOMELESSNESS:

The US rate of homelessness is twenty-one percent per 10,000 people, compared to thirty-one percent for veterans. During 2009 more than 136,000 veterans spent time in shelters; those on the streets were uncounted. A recent study counted 62,619 homeless veterans on a single night in January of 2012, of whom more than 5,000 were women. Eight percent of our homeless veterans every night are women, and their homelessness rate is more than double that of their nonveteran

---

[24] Ibid, 44.

peers. Seventy percent of homeless vets have psychological or substance-abuse problems.[25]

THE RESULTS OF A TRAUMATIC BRAIN INJURY STUDY:

The numbers of soldiers diagnosed with TBI keeps rising. A recent study suggests that as many as 320,000 troops have suffered some form of TBI. The study also raises the concern that 57 percent of those who reported possible brain injury had not seen a doctor for evaluation. Screenings for concussions are still not routinely done, so ruling out the presence of a concussion is a good starting place if symptoms indicative of TBI are noted.[26]

MILITARY SEXUAL TRAUMA (MST):

MST is usually perpetrated by another service member. Over 160,000 women have served in the current conflicts. Nearly one third of female veterans who seek help at VA facilities report having been a victim of rape or attempted rape while serving in the military. There is a growing awareness of military rapes perpetrated by males against males. Men

---

[25] Ibid, 48.
[26] John Sippola, Amy Blumenshine, Donald A. Tubesing, and Valerie Yancey. *Welcome Them Home Help Them Heal: Pastoral Care and Ministry with Service Members Returning from War.* (Minnesota: Whole Person Associates. 2009), 31.

who have been assaulted are at higher risk for substance abuse and suicide.[27]

STATISTICS FOR PTSD DISABILITY CLAIMS:

Considering disability claims alone, in my region PTSD disability claims from all veterans increased 300 percent from the start of the Iraq War to the present. Nationwide, VA claims increased almost 80 percent over five years—from 120,265 in 1999 to 215,871 in 2004. During the same period benefit payments jumped nearly 150 percent, from $1.72 billion to $4.28 billion. Disability and survivor benefits soared in 2007 to 81 percent above 2000 levels, increasing from $15.4 billion to a total of $34.3 billion. The VA predicts that these payments may increase to $59 billion by 2016.[28]

VETERAN UNEMPLOYMENT STATISTICS:

There is a high unemployment rate for recent war veterans, and according to the Department of Labor, as of summer 2005 the unemployment rate among the 3.9 million veterans was 5% higher than nonveterans. But young veterans ages 18 to 24 years old had an unemployment rate of almost 19%, double that of older

---

[27] Edward Tick. *War and the Soul: Healing Our Nation's Veterans from Post-traumatic Stress Disorder.* (Illinois: Theosophical Publishing House, 2005), 40.
[28] Ibid, 49.

veterans. By 2008 that rate rose to 19%, and by 2010 the employment rate for the same group surpassed 21%.[29]

At different times after I came back from Desert Storm and retired from the Army, I was searching to be around other veterans, especially women veterans. When I used to live near a military base, my doctor signed me up to participate in a female veterans support group, and it helped me get through the earlier months of my transition as a military retiree. Those days were really difficult because I was dealing with my loss of identity as an active duty soldier, which made me feel so proud that I served my country. I experienced a dramatic loss of income and benefits that affected my ability to provide for my family. Additionally, The VA was denying

---

[29] Ibid, 48.

the benefits I was applying for even though I qualified for them.

I will simply allow the statistics and studies to speak for themselves, as I have no desire to bad mouth the VA. Some veterans, including myself, experience great care from the VA. I truly just want to be an advocate for those veterans who have challenges with expressing their needs because they are physically injured, mentally challenged, and have damaged souls. WE need help. WE need more than medications for our bodies and minds. WE need healing for our souls, and that requires implementing spiritual and holistic medical care. Perhaps the VA or the federal government may someday consider more faith- based initiatives or alternate care as viable resources and will financially support and establish and build stronger veterans healing opportunities.

MY JOURNEY

TO

RESILIENCE

A few years prior to 2012, I felt like my mind was going crazy, so I kept busy with both of my sons' extra-curricular activities and started a community group in search of a support system like those on a military base. Near the middle of 2011, I felt God leading me to attend seminary, which led me to Palmer Theological Seminary to pursue a M.Div. degree. Feeling incompetent and overwhelmed by being a student, writing, and speaking in front of people, I changed my Master of Divinity (M. Div.) degree to a Master of Arts in Religion (MAR) degree. One of my classes was Spiritual Formation, and for the first time I was required to do some inner reflecting that had to be shared in writing assignments and classroom discussions.

Some painful memories about my war and military experiences surfaced, causing me to have some intense reactions within. Looking back, I am so thankful that I was in counseling at the vet center, where the opportunity to work through my triggers and emotions was available with a trained social worker. Once I told the class my status as a Desert Storm veteran, a male classmate shared with me in private that he was an Iraq war veteran. He expressed his hardships with adjusting to being home and not feeling like the person he used to be. I told him about the vet center, which provides free, confidential counseling to war veterans, and I shared my war challenges also.

After that, he was given resources to help him receive benefits. Knowing he was in the class helped me, because I had another veteran to talk with. During the semester in class, we read *Scarred by Struggle, Transformed by Hope*, by

Joan D. Chittister, and for the first time I understood that:

> the spirituality of struggle is, then, a spirituality that takes change and turns it into conversion, takes isolation and makes it independence, takes darkness and forms it into faith, takes the one step beyond fear to courage, takes powerlessness and reclaims it as surrender, takes vulnerability and draws out of it the freedom that comes with self-acceptance, faces the exhaustion and comes to value endurance for its own sake, touches the scars and knows them to be transformational.[30]

For my final assignment, I wrote: "My favorite class was Spiritual Formation. I learned more about the importance of doing inner work, which requires spiritual discipline to bring about self-discovery. I will continue my journey with God,

---

[30] Joan D. Chittister. *Scarred by Struggle, Transformed by Hope.* (Michigan: William B. Eerdmans Publishinng Company, 2003), 96.

who absolutely loves me for me- not for what I did or do."[31]

When Palmer Theological Seminary moved to King of Prussia, I transferred to LTSP and started classes in the fall. The course titled "Thinking About God" helped me to understand God as a healer and redeemer. It helped me to recognize more deeply His attributes and power. During the semester we learned many theology terms that helped me comprehend Christian language. For an assignment, we were required to read *Theological Language: Fullness of Silence* by Gustavo Gutierrez. In my reflection paper in response to that reading, I wrote:

> The theological perspective of Gutierrez implies that people suffer, and they need the help of others to assist them in order to get home through universal language

---

[31] Constance Cotton. "Spiritual Insight Assignment" (Palmer Theological Seminary, 2012).

and actions. Telling stories to stimulate hope and just listening and being in the presence of those who are oppressed makes a difference because people feel they aren't alone. Sometimes people are the only God others see.[32]

As I interact with other veterans, I take the time to listen to their stories to better understand their positive and negative military experiences. Sometimes veterans don't share those experiences with civilians, or even their families, because they feel that they will be judged or misunderstood. During my conversations with veterans, I normally share some resources to help them; I try to find a way to connect with them as a way of giving them hope.

I also completed the African-American Theology course, which significantly helped me embrace

---

[32] Constance Cotton, "Reflection Paper", (MAR Paper, LTSP, 2012).

my culture and identity in a positive, life-changing way.

Healing Opportunity in 2012

I joined an African American VFW Post and had the opportunity to be trained as a service officer, which gave me the knowledge to help veterans apply for their benefits. Also, I was given the task to assist with the planning and execution of a Veteran's Day event for the VFW. The post consisted of mainly Korean and Vietnam War veterans, with a few members from World War II and Desert Storm. Everyone was honored and received certificates from the New Jersey NAACP. In addition, young people participated, including my sons, by helping with the decorations, showcasing their talents, and being the honor guard. The war veterans felt validated, and we talked about the event for a long time. It was very special for me because I was able to use my logistics military training and practice the Event Coordinator skills I acquired in the Army.

Seminary Healing Journey in 2013

In the Spring Term at LTSP, I registered for The Black Presence in Scripture Course. Dr. Pollard was the professor, and he taught me about the contributions of people of color, also known as Blacks, African Americans, Africans, Colored, Negros, etc. He gave many resources to better understand our origin, culture, and varied religious backgrounds. At the end of the course, I felt worthy, significant, and more connected to many characters in the Bible. the course gave me a desire to seek more knowledge about my culture and our black history. I felt that God had fearfully and wonderfully made me, and He had a special purpose for my life despite the systematic oppression, racism, and injustice that is so prevalent toward people of color. A Marine veteran was in the class, and we shared our military and veteran journeys, which was very helpful to me.

Additionally, I registered for the Living Out A Faith Subversive of Injustice course, which was taught by Dr. Bloomquist. She exposed me to global injustices, government oppression, and marginalization. Sadly, I was able to identify how the military was a hurtful empire, and how it controlled service members. This made sense to me for the first time. For my final paper, I wrote about the injustices of women combat veterans.

Healing Opportunity in 2013

I went to the VA hospital for a Gulf War registry appointment. The Gulf War registry collects data from Gulf War veterans about their physical and mental health symptoms to establish the existence of presumptive illnesses and conditions that are associated with the Gulf War. I learned more information about Gulf War Illness, and the doctor confirmed that my medical issues were the same as thousands of other Gulf War veterans. For the first time, after seeing many physicians since 1991 who had very limited knowledge of Gulf War Illness, I felt understood by a doctor.

Some healing happened that day because the doctor validated that my concerns weren't "all in my head," like the VA assumed. Gulf War veterans suffer from medical issues like cognitive dysfunction, headaches, musculoskeletal pain, fatigue, respiratory problems, sleep disturbances, and dermatology issues. Gulf War veterans also have brain imaging abnormalities, and other disorders and complaints. I was still frustrated that, given the amount of money the government spends on Gulf War research, they are still not taking care of the medical and mental needs of Gulf War veterans.

Seminary Healing Journey in 2014

During the spring semester, I participated in an African American Church History course. The professor introduced me to Womanist theology, which is associated with Black feminism. The framework used for "Womanist theology includes practices, Biblical interpretation, traditions, and scriptures. Womanist theology is inclusive of all women of color and the focus is on liberation and empowerment."[33]

---

[33] Constance Cotton, "Womanist Theology: The Acknowledgement of Black Women's Experiences and Spirituality" (MAR Paper, LTSP, 2014).

Being an African American female has caused me to be subjected to sexism, classism, and racism in all aspects of my life, especially in the military. My gravitation to Womanist theology was immediate because it "…gives women of color the opportunity to share their experiences, value, and faith."[34] As a woman war veteran, safe spaces are barely provided, especially for African Americans, and "their experiences seem to be unappreciated and devalued so their stories often are not told."[35]

From a seminarian perspective, Womanist theology has given me the space to "delve deeper into the problematics of 'race' and to note its power and tenacity in political and academic

---

[34] Ibid,1.
[35] Ibid,4.

discourses."[36] Furthermore, as I inform other seminarians, in particular women of color, about my experience in the military, and the challenges of being a veteran, the information can "provide theologians with the contours and the vision to move ahead"[37] with addressing the needs of veterans. The stories of women veterans of color are essential, because "storytelling keeps our societal, spiritual, and cultural past and present in the forefront of our minds,"[38] especially in the black community.

Learning and embracing Womanist theology helped me reclaim my voice and realize that my story has significance. I suppressed my military

---

[36] Stacey Floyd-Thomas. *Deeper Shades of Purple: Womanism In Religion and Society* (New York,
   NY: New York University Press, 2006), 253.
[37] Ibid,268.
[38] Monica E. Coleman, *Making a Way Out of No Way: A Womanist Theology*, (Minneapolis, MN: Fortress
   Press, 2008), 105.

and veteran experiences to hide the pain, shame, and guilt. After the course I began to write about my journey and verbally share it, and I felt relieved to know that some people cared.

In the fall of 2014, I took an Introduction to Public Theology course taught by Professor Jon Paul. In the beginning of the course, the students had to choose a group based on a topic. I chose to be a part of a war group because I felt the need to bring awareness to what war veterans go through. The group was one of the first presenters during the course, and I had the pleasure of working with some fantastic students who brought an array of war experiences to present to the class. I was scared when my time came to speak, because I normally don't like to speak in front of people, and moreover, I didn't want to get too emotional about the material I was addressing.

I spoke about the war experiences of different veterans. I showed a YouTube clip of soldiers overseas in Iraq talking with their home church in the United States; it brought comfort to those soldiers knowing that they had their church body praying and supporting them during the war. I also shared my story of being in Desert Storm and the challenges I faced being a woman combat veteran. Near the end of my presentation, I couldn't speak anymore because of the overwhelming emotions I was feeling; I started crying. That was the first time that I publicly shared my story, and even though it was difficult, I can feel that some healing took place. Later, during the Public Theology course, Dr. Swain, who teaches pastoral care, shared her book called *Trauma and Transformation at Ground Zero: A Pastoral Theology* with the class. Her presentation was very moving, and she helped me understand the distress and grief that took place at Ground Zero. She revealed that people of different faiths came together to grieve and help those who were suffering. Talking about her experience at Ground Zero brought healing to me. Prior to that I really didn't talk about what happened at Ground Zero, because I associated Ground Zero with my Army Reserve unit being mobilized to go to Iraq, and the trauma that was associated with 9/11, which was a long-lasting trigger for me.

She also exposed us to an article she wrote titled "T. Mort. Chaplaincy at Ground Zero: Presence and Privilege on Holy Ground." Someone expressed the following in the article:

> This experience has scarred and changed my life. The horrendous loss of innocent life, the depth of pain and suffering for survivors, and the long-term recovery work that remains to be done over the months and years to come are awesome. It is a shame that it takes so much pain, so much death, to bring out the good that we have seen here among the people of New York, and the thousands who have come to help. At least we know of what we are capable. It's just too bad what had to happen in order to see that good blossoms in real life rather than just in words.[39]

I was reminded of my time in the war when we had to deal with so many hardships, deaths, and injuries. However, as military personnel, we did humanitarian efforts and good deeds to help others during chaos. As a part of the course we had to visit another faith community, and I chose to visit a mosque in the area where I live.

---

[39] Storm Swain. *The T. Mort Chaplaincy at Ground Zero: Presence and Privilege on Holy Ground.* (New York: Springer Publishing Company, 2011), 4.

Prior to the visit, Muslims scared me, because we were surrounded by Muslims in Saudi Arabia and at times, they caused us harm. After I came back from war, I had a doctor's appointment at the VA and my doctor was a Muslim who wore a head wrap. I was so petrified of him that I was not able to complete my doctor appointment.

My visit to the mosque ended up being just what I needed to help me overcome some of my fears about Muslims. They gave me a warm welcome and ensured that I felt comfortable for the duration of the service. Then the message was given by the Imam, and it was about the way the news media depicts Muslims and Islam as terroristic. He expressed that there is no such thing as an Islam extremist. He thought that some Muslims may have extremist behavior, but they are not Islam extremists. The messenger went on to say that Islam has pockets of Muslims who are harmful, but for the most part Islam is about peace, love and unity. He encouraged us to have a global view, because we are not here just for ourselves; we are called to serve mankind. Surprisingly, I enjoyed my visit to the mosque. They invited me to return even though they knew that I was a Christian. I noticed more commonalities in the way we practice our spiritual disciplines and traditions. They expressed love to one another and used scriptures for guidance and understanding.

IN MY

OWN

WORDS

I believe God is calling me to educate people about veterans as a form of public theology, and to provide resources to churches which can assist the veterans and their congregations in communities. Furthermore, my ability to collaborate with organizations will hopefully build relationships that will create veteran-based events and opportunities. Taking the Public Theology class confirmed that my voice matters. Attending chapel before class was strongly suggested during the semester. My sentiments about the experience were written in my Public Theology final paper, which says, "One day I was asked if I would be willing to volunteer at chapel and I said yes. Another student at the seminary, who is going to school to become a Chaplain in the Army National Guard, volunteered to work with me, which was very comforting. We led worship together. She said the prayers and some of the liturgy, and I selected and read the Scriptures and chose the songs. The chapel service was special for me because I worked with someone in the military and had a chance to connect with her as we prepared and practiced. Also, being a part of a service that remembered veterans touches my heart, because I was practicing public theology. I was nervous about the idea of leading chapel, but God allowed me to push beyond my fear to be theologically engaged in honoring veterans for their service and sacrifice. Veterans deserve to be helped and ministered to because they need the support of society to make America a safe place for them. May God bless America and the veterans who fought for America's freedom. The Public Theology course was instrumental in helping me understand the importance of caring for others. I realized that God doesn't waste pain. One of the scriptures that stood out to me during that semester is second Corinthians 1:4–5, which says, "Blessed be the God and father of our Lord Jesus Christ, the father of mercies, and the God of all comfort; who comforts us in all our tribulation, that we may be able to come for them which are in any trouble by the comfort wherewith we ourselves are comforted of God."[40]

Healing Opportunities in 2014

In March, I went to Women Veterans Rock, which was the first female veteran event I attended. The event was held at Chestnut Hill College, and many women from all branches of the service attended. Some were active duty, some reservists, and some veterans. Other women there were civilians who worked for the

---

[40] Constance Cotton, "Introduction to Public Theology" (Final Paper, LTSP, 2014).

government. Workshops were offered to us, and some of the topics included women's health, becoming an entrepreneur, and finding balance. I interacted with some wonderful women, and we shared our military journey with one another. Connecting with other female veterans was a source of healing for me because I could relate to them. We were given the opportunity to talk to a spiritual advisor, and I signed up. The lady I spoke with really took the time to listen to my concerns, and she provided me with some needed resources. She encouraged me to continue my therapy sessions at the vet center, and she prayed for me.

During October, my Township unveiled a wall of honor that displayed photos and stories of veterans who were associated with the town. My picture and military history were presented, and they allowed me to honor my father also, whose picture and military service are located next to mine. The local newspaper reporter interviewed my father and me, and our stories were in the newspaper the following day. I felt so special, because my neighborhood took the time to thank us for our service. The wall of honor was done in excellence, and my dad and I experienced a very special moment together.

My counseling appointments at the Vet Center increased, so I was able to work through more issues that were suppressed. My social worker encouraged me to share my story when she invited me to be on a panel of veterans at an event designed for civilians to better understand the challenges of war veterans. At times, it was difficult to answer peoples' questions, but as time went on I became more transparent which gave them more insight about my struggles and resilience. Afterwards, the feeling of appreciation overwhelmed me. The veterans who were also on the panel encouraged and accepted one another, which was a blessing.

Seminary Healing Journey in 2015

In January of 2015, The War and the Christian Conscience course was the hardest one for me to get through. For the first time, I was introduced to terms like pacifists, just and unjust war, noncombatants and combatants, and proportionality, which means accessing the collateral damage done to civilians and military personnel as it relates to war. As a combat veteran, listening to the different theories was a challenge because my experience in war was incongruent to what some of the theories were expressing. When I was in the military, I didn't take the time to understand if the war was just or unjust, because I was trained to follow orders and fight during war. In hindsight, my exposure to some of the language and terms taught in the course would have changed my perspective of staying in the military.

Unfortunately, I experienced a lot of triggers during the course. We were required to give a presentation in class. My topic was on the proportionality of individuals during Desert Shield/Desert Storm, which included real life stories of U.S. soldiers, devastating statistics, and graphic videos. For my final paper, I wrote about the women combat veterans. Here are some of the stories about four military women who were the first women to accomplish recognition for their contributions from the paper:

Shoshana Johnson was the first female African American prisoner of war (POW). She endured bullet injuries to both of her ankles, which did not heal properly during her captivity. In March of 2003, the soldiers were ambushed, and "It would be months after the ambush and capture of Shoshana Johnson and her fellow soldiers before Donald Rumsfeld and the Bush administration would even acknowledge that we were fighting an insurgency."[41] Former Marine Captain Vernice Armour was the first African American female combat pilot who served during the invasion of Iraq in 2003. Captain Armour "helped ensure the safety of Marines and soldiers on the ground by seeking out and attacking the enemy from the cockpits of her F-

---

[41] Shoshana Johnson and M. L. Doyle. *I'm Still Standing: From Captive U.S. Soldier to Free Citizen- My Journey Home.* (New York: Simon & Schuster, 2010), ix.

18 fighter jet and Cobra attack helicopter."[42] Another woman, "Army Sergeant Leigh Ann Hester, became the first women since World War II to be awarded the Silver Star medal for valor in combat for leading soldiers in a counterattack after 50 insurgents ambushed an area they were guarding."[43] Second Lieutenant Perez was the first African American female officer to be killed in combat, and the first West Point female graduate to lose her life in the Iraq War. Emily Perez, a Cadet Command Sergeant Major, graduated from The United States Military Academy at West Point as the first minority woman to hold that position. She died at the age of 23.

---

[42] Kirsten Holmstedt. *Band Of Sisters: American Women War in Iraq*. (Pennsylvania: Stackpole Books, 2007), 311
[43] Ibid, 309.

Sadly, many women lost their lives during the recent wars, and:

> numerous women warriors died from non-combat related deaths; military authorities still have some of their cases under investigation. At 19 years old, Lavena Johnson's death made her the first woman to die in the wars in Afghanistan and Iraq. The military has the death listed as a suicide; however, her father, a doctor and military veteran, was suspicious about this, so he did his own research. As he looked further into her case, he read military records and viewed pictures; he and others believe she was murdered. According to news reports, she had teeth marks, bruises, and scratches on her body. Additionally, a chemical to burn her vagina area was present to cover up the fact that she may have been raped, which was noted in her file. Furthermore, the military autopsy revealed she had broken teeth, a broken lip, a broken nose, and a gunshot wound incongruent to a suicide ruling. Moreover, PFC Johnson's body was found in a contractor's tent with a trail of blood going away from the tent. Someone tried to burn down the tent with her dead body in it.[44]

---

[44] Love, David. "Lavena Johnson: Raped and Murdered on a Military Base in Iraq" http://www.alternet.org (accessed March 20, 2016).

Often when women die in combat, the media doesn't publicize their stories. Because of this, military families as well as female veterans and active duty personnel can "feel there is a segment of America that wants to hide the fact that women die in combat operations, almost as if they are ashamed, they have put women in such a position."[45] Women volunteer for an array of reasons to serve their country in peace and war time. So far, in the recent wars, "more than seventy American women have been killed on the battlefield."[46] Female warriors suffered from the wounds of wars too, just like their male counterparts. In recent wars, "More than 430 female warriors have been wounded in

---

[45] Kirsten Holmstedt. *Band Of Sisters: American Women at War in Iraq*. (Pennsylvania: Stackpole Books, 2007), 312.

[46] Ibid, 309.

combat."⁴⁷ While fighting in the Iraq War, "Army Corporal Rachelle Spors received the Purple Heart for the wounds she received and was a patient at various hospitals in Iraq and in the States."⁴⁸

Writing my paper about women war veterans was difficult, but I pushed through the pain because I wanted their stories told, and I felt the need to dedicate my paper to them in recognition of their service, sacrifice, and duty for America's freedom. For many months after taking the War and Christian Conscience Course, I had some mental and physical setbacks because of the course content, requirements, and discussions. However, I don't regret taking the course, due to the healing that later emerged.

---

⁴⁷ Ibid, 309.
⁴⁸ Ibid, 319.

Simultaneously, I enrolled in another course titled "Race, Gender, Sexuality, and Leadership" which was taught by Professor Karyn Wiseman. We learned about the challenges associated with racism, gained a better understanding of the LBGTQ community, and discussed gender issues in society including the oppression and disrespect of women. I had the opportunity to give a presentation about women in the military and wrote a paper on developing a retreat for women veterans. I really enjoyed this class because it was engaging, very interactive, and addressed real life experiences.

During the fall semester, my participation in the Baptist Polity course, taught by Dr. Croft, was enlightening. Even though I am a member of a Baptist church, my knowledge about Baptist beliefs, policy, and practice was very limited. The opportunity to understand and assess my decision of being affiliated with the Baptist denomination was challenged and validated. We were required to write a paper on baptism, which helped me for the first time to articulate my experience. I wrote:

My baptism experience was at Christian Stronghold Baptist Church in 1991. I started going to church there after the war since I was taking a Christian counseling course at that location. A special feeling led me to join the church during the Thanksgiving service, which prompted me go to the altar for salvation and church membership. I accepted Jesus Christ as my personal Savior at my neighbor's house when I was seven, and had a relationship with God, but the war left me devastated, so I thought I needed to rededicate my life to God. I desired membership with a church where I could spiritually grow. Loneliness, and not being the same person as I was before war, made me feel isolated. My family and friends misunderstood me, and I had difficulties assimilating back into society with PTSD and war- related medical problems. Desert Storm was the first war that females were engaged in, and society- including the government -wasn't equipped to help us when we returned home. As a matter of fact, the Veterans Administration told Gulf War veterans that our symptoms were "all in our heads" for about fifteen years and didn't provide medical care for us. Around 2009, the Veterans Administration finally declared that Gulf War Illness is real.[49]

A war veteran's perspective

---

[49] Cotton, Constance. "Baptism Paper." (MAR Paper, LTSP 2015).

Baptism was significant to my healing; I needed to get closer to God, since I experienced what felt like hell during the war. I felt betrayed by the government, and unforgiven for the things I did directly or indirectly during Desert Storm. Before attending Christian Stronghold Baptist Church, I thought baptism was another way people became saved, but they taught me differently. My baptism experience is so memorable; I felt like a changed person. In some ways, I felt accepted by the Church even though I experienced some tough situations in the military and dealt with some unimaginable circumstances in the war.

Furthermore, "in A Baptist Manual of Polity and Practice, my baptism experience was articulated well when the author" expressed that "by an oath a soldier pledges his loyal service to a nation, and wearing a uniform identifies him as one committed to such special service. Likewise, baptism is a means in which we yield ourselves to God, and the fact that it is done publicly makes it a sign to the world that we are members of Christ's church."[50]

We also had to write about the Lord's Supper. I reflected on the observance of the Lord's Supper at Enon Tabernacle Baptist Church, where my family has been members for over ten years. In the paper I shared my Communion experiences at Bethany Baptist Church, Christian Stronghold Baptist Church, and Enon. My sentiments expressed that "the Lord's Supper reminds me that God is inclusive, and Communion is the time when everyone who is present is acknowledged and respected

---

[50] Ibid,1.

collectively and not judged. People seem to be more patient and loving towards one another, and the congregation feels unified."[51] Because I am a war veteran, the aforementioned makes me feel accepted and gives me comfort. Additionally, the Lord's Supper may "be the means through which the Holy Spirit speaks and acts while our faith is increased and strengthened."[52]

Understanding the Four Baptist Freedoms, which are Bible freedom, soul freedom, church freedom, and religious freedom, helped me have a special appreciation for the Baptist tradition. Various churches have helped me over the years. Most of the congregations knew that I was a war veteran experiencing emotional and physical pain from my combat experience. No

---

[51] Ibid, 3.
[52] [52] Norman H. Maring and Winthrop S. Hudson. *A Baptist Manual of Polity and Practice*. Rev. ed. (Valley Forge: Judson Press, 1991) 153.

one discerned my desire to commit suicide because of my mental anguish, isolation, and medical problems. I wish they had a veterans ministry so I could be among other comrades who understood my language and experiences.

Healing Opportunities in 2015

My first time visiting Cranaleith Spiritual Center was around April, and it was so special because I had the occasion to meet other women veterans in a beautiful setting. The program was focused on women veterans. We related to one another, and since then we have been at different women veteran events together. I met the founder of the Women's Veteran Center, and to my surprise she was a Desert Storm veteran too. We shared our war experiences and some of the concerns we had for veterans. Today, we continue to stay in touch and support one another. Cranaleith created a place and space for healing, self-discovery, and spirituality, as we discussed and worked through some exercises individually and collectively.

The Catholic Sisters who work at Cranaleith intentionally asked us questions to help stimulate a dialogue about our life experiences as women, as well as veterans, in a way that helped us locate where we were at that moment in our faith journey. Additionally, they gave us time to unwind and think about ourselves in a deeper reflective way, which helped us to assess ourselves and talk about our relationship with God. We built an altar and each of us was given an opportunity to write our prayer request on a piece of paper and place it in a beautiful bowl that was at the altar. The sisters prayed over our concerns. Before leaving, we took pictures together and exchanged contact information. A Cranaleith staff member informed us that they will plan another retreat for women veterans, and the Sisters of Mercy encouraged us to keep in touch with them.

In early October, I went to an AMVETS women veterans retreat hosted by Nancy McGory Richardson who is the founder of Freedom and Honor. The participants were assigned rooms and I had the pleasure of having a Desert Storm veteran as a roommate. We talked a lot about our experiences in the war, and we discovered we had duty assignments in the same areas. As war veterans, we discussed our challenges. The retreat gave us opportunities to heal in large and small group sessions. Some topics were difficult because they required us to talk about pain most of us suppressed. At the end, we exchanged contact information and expressed our gratitude for a safe and confidential space to tell our stories and focus on ourselves, which brought about healing. The retreat positively changed my life.

From October 20 -22, I attended a workshop titled "Tending Moral Injury After War: A Workshop for Faith Leaders" at Cranaleith Spiritual Center in Philadelphia. The instructor was Rev. Chris J. Antal, who was a chaplain in the Iraq and Afghanistan wars. My female friend who is a Desert Storm veteran attended the event with me, and to my surprise a female veteran from LTSP was there also. A Sister of Mercy and a civilian who experienced war in Africa were also present. We were asked to bring in an item that reminded us of the war, so we could put it on the alter we created. I brought a magazine that addressed the damaging effects of the Gulf War Illness, since I suffer from medical and mental problems that stem from it. We had opportunities to work through different situations and scenarios to get a better understanding of moral and soul injury. Attending the workshop gave me language to describe what I had been feeling for years. Before, I felt unforgiven and betrayed. To experience the workshop with others who experienced some form of war was a blessing, and God allowed me to be healed from some of the effects of war. I was able to share my struggles in a safe and confidential environment.

Rev. Antal talked about the definition and symptoms of Post-Traumatic Stress Disorder (PTSD). After he was finished, I remembered reading in a book that "PTSD is not a 'disorder,' as the American Psychiatric Association has labeled it. Instead, it is an injury; a war injury. This injury includes a 'destruction of the capacity for social trust.' This destruction is necessary for survival in war, but it prevents one from reincorporating into society at home."[53]

Women war veterans shared their stories about the effects of PTSD. Sergeant Katharine Broome, who was in the Virginia Army National Guard during the war, conveyed that her PTSD affects her life, and that "the whole experience is with me everywhere I go. I can't leave it behind. It's in every new relationship I build. It's affected every old relationship I had."[54] Specialist Elizabeth Sartain, who served in the U. S. Army, said "I'm angry. I didn't have this PTSD before

---

[53] [53]Laura Browder. *When Janey Comes Marching Home: Portraits of Women Combat Veterans.* (North Carolina: University of North Carolina Press, 2010), 153.
[54] Ibid, 124.

deployment, and it's a career-ender for me. There are a lot of people who have it, but they're two years away from retirement, so they don't get help."[55]

Rev. Antal exposed us to the books written by his friend Ed Tick, and in *War and the Soul: Healing Our Nation's Veterans from Post-Traumatic Stress Disorder*, he makes this observation:

Until recently, few of us knew about such a thing as Post-Traumatic stress. The veteran and his family (for most of the wars until the Gulf War, vets were mainly men) were left to make the journey through the labyrinth of behaviors and feelings on their own, with little support or understanding of the territory they were to travel. Once home, many veterans and their families were faced with the daily challenge of trying to negotiate and avoid the triggers that drew out the invisible demons: the memories and past experiences that continue to impact a

---

[55] Ibid, 23.

vet's behavior and ability to live tranquilly in the civilian world.[56]

Rev. Antal shared very detailed information about soul and moral injury. His published work explains the need for veterans services in the church:

> ...the increasing number of returning veterans in our churches and communities signal a growing need for clergy and religious educators to assess the pastoral concerns and requirements that these veterans and their families may be facing. Military professionals now warn of the real danger of spiritual and moral trauma. We are only now beginning to understand the true impact of war and violence on those called to fight, and those for whom they fight. These women and men have been taught to be violent. Yet when they return home, they are not taught how to unlearn violence. Unmasking violence is hard to do when our veterans are reliving their experiences of violence daily.[57]

---

[56] Edward Tick. *War and the Soul: Healing Our Nation's Veterans from Post-traumatic Stress Disorder.* (Illinois: Theosophical Publishing House, 2005), 67.
[57] Chris J. Antal. *Moral Injury, Soul Repair, and Creating a Place for Grace.* (Religious Education, Vol. 110, No. 4, 2012), 382.

Rev. Antal helped me understand that the military defends the nation, and military personnel volunteered with the hope of protecting their country for noble and just causes. Listening to him, I was also reminded that "for the military to function efficiently, it must run on a hierarchy of power, tradition, and discipline. Basic training curtails our personal will, and then brutal combat damages or destroys it as we are forced to act in ways that oppose our civilized natures and established identities."[58] During and after the war, many veterans could have realized that they were fighting for people's greed and power, not for freedom; they also were fighting to stay alive. Some soldiers may feel betrayed by the

---

[58] Edward Tick. *War and the Soul: Healing Our Nation's Veterans from Post-traumatic Stress Disorder* (Illinois: Theosophical Publishing House, 2005), 19.

government, especially when they realize that their own government caused intentional harm to them by exposing them to toxic environments and harmful health problems associated with Agent Orange and the Gulf War Illness. To add insult to injury, military personnel had to fight for their benefits, which should be easily given to them. Interestingly, "In every war, up to and including the present one in Iraq, politicians and military leaders have sought to mobilize their people by reminding them that they are engaging in war under divine order and protection."[59] Based on the trauma and devastation experienced by war veterans, some veterans feel guilt, shame, and remorse for their direct and indirect actions during war. After September 11, 2001, "the unimaginable tragedy mobilized

---

[59] Ibid, 42.

many young men and women who wanted to serve their country and go after the terrorists who had inflicted so much pain on the United States."[60] Military personnel were willing to die, yet many came back home unprepared to pay the cost of continued existence; they now face the challenges of moral and soul injury, PTSD, and other trials that no one told them about.

In November, Senator Vincent Hughes honored women veterans at a high school in Philadelphia, PA. Upon entering the event, the hosts made us feel welcome, and they guided the participants to the auditorium. The high school students performed a memorable military -themed show, and singers and speakers acknowledged us in a meaningful way. The students lined up to give

---

[60] Dava Guerin and Kevin Ferris. *Unbreakable Bonds: The Mighty Moms and Wounded Warriors of Walter Reed.* (New York: Skyhorse, 2014) 95.

us roses, and they honored all the branches of the military by playing our respective anthems. Afterwards, a documentary was presented about the contributions of colored women in the military. Next, we were led upstairs and treated to a delicious meal. I interacted with many women veterans and shared some resources with them. Senator Vincent Hughes gave us certificates and time to take pictures with him. The hosts genuinely cared about all the women who served their country. I felt special, respected, and valued.

Healing Opportunities in 2016

On March 17, 2016, I was invited to be a keynote speaker by Cathy Santos, who is the founder of National Alliance of Women Veterans, Inc., at the fifth annual Women Veterans Pray located at the Philadelphia Veterans Hospital Heroes Chapel. I felt very honored to speak to other women veterans; it was a healing opportunity for me. It was such a blessing to worship God with my fellow female comrades. We shared our stories about being in the military and the challenges and blessings of being a veteran.

One veteran who attended served during the Vietnam Era, and she angrily told her story about suffering from Agent Orange and breast cancer, and about how the VA turned her away for medical care because they didn't have the resources to treat her as a woman veteran. The woman was also a military sexual trauma victim. Since it was women's history month, a male veteran acknowledged the first African-American female who joined the military in 1866; her name was Cathy Williams. Female VA Chaplains were also a part of the program. Every woman present had a chance to share whatever they wanted, which made the event very special to me, because it was inclusive, and everyone was affirmed. I invited an old friend of mine from Scotland School for Veterans Children who works at the VA, and to my surprise she was able to attend the entire time. She is a veteran also, and recently shared her medical challenges with me. She is having problems getting her VA benefits even though she is a VA employee.

During my speech I encouraged the women to take better care of themselves. I emphasized the importance of moving forward with God every day. I reminded them that despite the suffering we go through in life, God is a healer, and able to help us through our trials and tribulations. For the first time I wasn't nervous speaking in front of a crowd, because I knew my female comrades understood and embraced me. After the service, female veterans showed interest in having more spiritual events to help them heal.

On March 26, 2016, I attended Operation: I Am Woman, A Women Veteran Symposium at Camden County College in Blackwood, NJ. At the registration table one of the sponsors of the event checked me in, and I expressed my gratitude for their hosting and recognizing women veterans. The only workshop I attended was about resiliency, and the presenter was Catherine Williams, an Army veteran who served 7 years in the medical field. She currently works full-time assisting veterans at the Department of

Behavioral and Intellectual Disability Services in Philadelphia, PA. Her presentation captured the harsh realities of women currently serving in the military and women veterans as she discussed current statistics and the lack of support available. However, she also shared resources and ideas to assist with becoming resilient, and encouraged us to tell our stories, advocate for our needs, and develop support systems. Later, we ate lunch and interacted with attendees and various vendors who represented military service organizations and resources.

The last activity on the agenda was the Bridging the Gap Forum Panel, which gave us the space to ask questions and share our concerns. Some of the panelists included a Desert Storm veteran who started a women veteran non-profit organization, an Air Force veteran who is employed by the federal government and helping veterans with MST, PTSD, and substance abuse, and an Air Force female war veteran who serves as a civilian military readjustment counselor at the Vet Center.

We had a lot of questions and comments, but some topics resonated with me more. Most topics that were discussed saddened me, because I could feel the pain and suffering. We talked about the divide between those who are combat and peacetime veterans, the different branches of service that can cause service members to be treated unfairly, benefits and services based on the length of service, and the dissimilar treatment of female enlisted soldiers and officers whom women veterans contend with. I'm glad we addressed that, because women veterans can get hurt by those divisive categories; it can make our journey to assist all female veterans counterproductive. As usual, we didn't have enough time to address everyone's concerns.

Some women talked about their military sexual trauma and how devastated they are. One woman conveyed her dislike that only certain wars are mentioned, and she started naming other wars like the Cold War, Bosnia, and Kosovo that people don't talk about. She also talked about the wars within the military that females fight such as sexism, racism, and discrimination. Another woman veteran chimed in and expressed that females need someone to protect them from the military while they are serving, and that she felt like collateral damage. One of the panelists shared that women can experience PTSD from not only war, but some other traumatic events which can be prevalent, and the symptoms don't always show up right away.

A female veteran was concerned about homeless veterans and wanted to know what we are doing to take the services to the street; all vets are not competent to seek help, and some veterans don't want to be housed and cared for because of fear and intimidation. Another panelist informed us that her job sends workers on the street to help veterans. An Army veteran suggested that we tell the media our stories, to spread the word about women veteran needs and challenges, and to advocate for services for us.

Panelists gave us the history of the Vet Center; they let us know that it came about by the demands of Vietnam veterans wanting a safe place to address their military needs. Once it was established, it became a separate entity from the VA to ensure confidentiality. At the VA, veterans' medical and mental health information can be shared or can become an open book to any provider treating a veteran, which makes many veterans uncomfortable with receiving care from the VA. At the end of the Women Veterans Symposium, we were given gifts, flags, and certificates, and we happily marched in a big circle to military- themed music. I had some meaningful conversations with the ladies present and reconnected with some women veterans I met before. Some healing took place for me, and I was reminded that women veterans are also seeking wholeness and comradery with their peers. The host is planning to have a similar event annually.

SUPPORTING VETERANS

Veterans need the attention, cooperation, and support of the whole society to heal. In 2013, I was going through a lot of stress with parenting two teenage sons, meeting the demands of my household, being a seminary student, and coping with my medical and mental health problems. I desired to be in a support group again, but I couldn't find one for female veterans, so I joined a male war veteran support group that mainly had Vietnam veterans present. At first, everything went smoothly, and the men welcomed me. They were nice guys. Eventually, after weeks of participating, some of the men made comments that I was being too emotional after sharing my challenges to the group. Also, as a Desert Storm veteran, my combat issues didn't seem to matter as much as the Vietnam War experiences. I stopped attending the meetings and was hoping to find a women war veteran support group or another veterans group where I felt comfortable.

Many veterans like me want opportunities to be around their comrades. Being a veteran can be lonely and overwhelming as we navigate society to find purpose and provision for our lives. Veterans are accustomed to being in structured settings that have some form of support on an ongoing basis when they served in the military. Unfortunately, those structures are not as readily accessible to veterans as they were when they were in the service. Veterans overall feel more comfortable around other veterans, because they can share their struggles and ask one another for help. Because of this, faith organizations can assist veterans by creating veterans ministries. It can be imperative to offer veterans "the spiritual strength to withstand adversity and to achieve one's goal."[61]

Over the last couple of months, I asked veterans and civilians I know if their faith organizations had a veterans ministry, and all of them replied no. One day while I was at LTSP, I briefly interviewed Dr. Quintin L. Robertson, who is the Director of the Urban Theological Institute at LTSP. In addition to that role, he serves as the interim pastor at Grace Baptist Church of Germantown in Philadelphia, PA. I asked the following questions:

Dr. Robertson

Does Grace Baptist Church of Germantown have a veterans ministry?

---

[61] B. Carter and M. McGoldrick. *The Expansive Family Life Cycle: Individual, Family, and Social Perspectives, 4th ed.* (New York: Allyn & Bacon, 2010).

Dr. Robertson: No, we do not, but we do recognize the veterans who are members of the church for Veteran's Day.

Do you think your church should have a veterans ministry? If so, who would oversee it?

Dr. Robertson: I think there is a need for one. Most likely it would fall under the community center or social affairs.

Do you think it should be open to non-members to give them opportunities to serve?

Dr. Robertson: I think it should be in reach and outreach, so the community can be involved also.

Constance: I didn't think about non-members of faith organizations being a part of the veterans ministry. That's a great idea because military families and other supporters can help veterans too.[62]

My interview with Dr. Robertson broadened my perspective and ideology about the importance of having a veterans ministry. One of the first steps faith organizations can do is identify veterans in their congregations and communities. Then, veterans should be informed that they have an opportunity to have a veterans ministry. By doing so, "the veterans will know it's specifically for them, and it will be a place where others understand their concerns, challenges and language."[63] Then, a meeting should be established with them to discuss where they can meet and available times. Additionally, veterans

---

[62] Dr. Quintin Robertson, interviewed by author, LTSP, March 29, 2016.
[63] Constance Cotton, "Creating a Veterans Ministry at Enon Tabernacle Baptist Church" (MAR Paper, LTSP, 2012).

should be told about any resources that are available and ways the faith organization can provide support.

When the veterans ministry is established, it's helpful to let the veterans involved determine their needs and issues, because people can have false assumptions or totally misunderstand veterans' needs and problems. Some veterans require or have caregivers. The veterans ministry can assist the caregivers of veterans by linking them to programs that offer caregiving training and compensation as they care for veterans. Oftentimes, veterans know about resources or can tell other veterans how to pursue their entitlements to housing, employment, healthcare, and education. Veterans ministries can be an asset to faith organizations because they can bring diversity and cross-cultural lines, since veterans are "accustomed to working and living with service members from different ethnicities, social classes, and education levels."[64]

Veterans "may have developed mental health issues during the time they served in the armed forces. Some veterans have been sexually assaulted, endured violent acts by other military personnel, fought in wars, or experienced traumatic events in the military."[65] A veterans ministry can provide a safe and confidential environment for them because "a community that is aware and intentional about being a resource for wholeness must create new structures in which members will share responsibility for healing activities in a more

---

[64]Ibid, 4.
[65]Ibid, 7.

inclusive and participatory way."⁶⁶

Furthermore, a veterans ministry would allow more opportunities for veterans to interact with one another:

"...those of us who have served in past military conflicts have an obligation to continue that service by being there now for our younger veterans. It's not about selling them our experiences, but rather listening to theirs. Even though the generations may be distant, there is an automatic bond among those who have worn the uniform. The best mentoring lets them know they are not alone and not crazy. There is nothing more rewarding than seeing the light come back on in the eyes of a younger soldier

---

[66] M.Z Kornfeld, *Cultivating Wholeness* (London: Continuum or Bloomsbury Academic, 2000), 40.

who knows he has found the trailhead to a more peaceful life."[67]

My purpose in writing this book is to show my full support to veterans across the globe. Of course, The VA can only help those who served in the US Armed Forces, but as a Christian I have a heart for all military servants who have experienced the trauma of war. Veterans deserve the best care available both mentally and physically. Their families, friends, and sometimes communities are affected, and Americans need to have more dialogue about the grieving and challenges that are occurring. Veterans were accustomed to having access to chaplains and chaplain assistance while serving in the military. They also had worship services of

---

[67] Edward Tick. *War and the Soul: Healing Our Nation's Veterans from Post-traumatic Stress Disorder.* (Illinois: Theosophical Publishing House, 2005), 232.

different denominations and religions available to them during peace and war time. Faith organizations can help by providing veterans ministries that can assist veterans in their congregations and community, because:

> Spirituality has been a healing force through countless generations, embedded in culture and religious traditions. For many people, spiritual beliefs can influence how to deal with life's stressful events and pain, and it can offer hope and resilience in times of adversity. Spiritual beliefs can be a powerful resource for people who have lost their way, are feeling despair, or are suffering from oppression, racism, poverty, and trauma.[68]

This is necessary because veterans, especially those who return home from war:

> ...realize that re-integration is a challenge because society has not shown interest, taken time, made space, opened their hearts, listened to stories, allowed veterans to grieve, admitted responsibility, shared burdens, adjusted expectations, or provided opportunities aligned with

---

[68] B. Carter and M. McGoldrick. *The Expansive Family Life Cycle: Individual, Family, and Social Perspectives, 4th ed.* (New York: Allyn & Bacon, 2010), 133.

military experience. The path to re-integration is for families, communities, and our society to reverse these issues. These could constitute a welcome home that would work.[69]

Although service organizations like the Veterans of Foreign Wars (VFW) and the American Legion are helpful, veterans ministries can serve as a place of healing:

> Because military personnel served at the behest of the nation, their redemption must happen in context of a "tribe.". When warriors "buy back their souls," they return to their bodies, minds, and hearts- their lives. But the task is not theirs alone; that constitutes betrayal. Society must "buy back" its warriors. The well-being of warriors and their societies are inseparable. Many of our veterans remain homeless in spirit… Communities must redeem their warriors, and lost honor must be restored in public eyes.[70]

---

[69] Edward Tick. *Warrior's Return: Restoring the Soul After War*. (Colorado: Sounds True, 2014), 229.

[70] Ibid, 237-238.

Prior military personnel involved in the veterans ministry can serve by being active members of their faith organizations and give to others. "The experience of listening to the veterans' first-person narratives of war is one that challenges prevailing cultural attitudes, social practices, and personal views about self, others, war, and interhuman connections. This experience is a transformational journey."[71] When the veterans ministry is a part of the faith organization, "others can provide key elements for coping with the trauma by using preaching, memory work, forgiveness, and grief counseling. While these certainly are not the only elements that can be offered to people struggling from the effects of trauma, they are essentials that are often overlooked in the process of caring for

---

[71] Ibid, 223.

individuals coping with the aftermath of trauma."[72]

The congregations can schedule prayer breakfasts, retreats, healing services, military-themed liturgy, and Bible studies that focus on God's love, mercy, and forgiveness. Those spiritual occasions can help war veterans because as combatants, veterans may feel that they participated in destroying the world. Through atonement practices they make it one again. Veterans might also live with grief, guilt, and shame. To restore their psyches in the world, they and their families can help give back what they demolished. Restoration practices can

---

[72] Schneider, Eugene William III. "Practical Pastoral Care: Observations from a Military Chaplain in Dealing with Trauma" (PhD diss., Lutheran Theological Seminary Philadelphia, 2009), 3.

be aligned with spiritual and religious teachings from both East and West.[73]

Veterans, mainly women veterans, should share their stories as much as possible so others can better understand who they are, what they did in the military, and their unmet needs. I feel misunderstood and frustrated about being a female war veteran at times, because people have their assumptions and ideologies. Some of my greatest healing moments have come from the times I interacted with other veterans and military families. Veterans tend to talk about their difficult military experiences with one another, particularly about war. Tick has this to say about civilians' behavior toward veterans: "…many of us might not confront the warrior because we don't want to add to the hurt. Other

---

[73] Ibid, 229.

times, we are apprehensive, afraid we might ignite their already short fuse. A lose/lose situation begins to develop, and the relationship gap grows wider."[74]

I'm grateful that God has truly kept me and given me healing moments. My husband's and sons' ongoing love has provided me with a safe and stable support system which has helped me become resilient. My parents' availability and consistency, especially during tough times, always made me know I was loved, which has fueled my courage to keep moving forward. My sister's love, support, and willingness to listen and give me good advice has helped me realize that my painful struggles need to be expressed so that I can experience hope and

---

[74] Edward Tick. *War and the Soul: Healing Our Nation's Veterans from Post-traumatic Stress Disorder.* (Illinois: Theosophical Publishing House, 2005), 103.

transformation. God has blessed me with many encouragers who helped me persevere when I wanted to give up. Unlike myself, some veterans don't have support systems, which perpetuates the negative outcomes they deal with. Veterans ministries, as well as other resources, can provide advocacy for their needs and foster accountability. Too many veterans are struggling and dying. Veterans and their loved ones can benefit from spiritual guidance and support to help them cope with life in society. Veterans need help with experiencing a good quality of life; at least they should have their basic needs met in a way that is similar to what they had in the military. Faith organizations and their commitment to provide veterans ministries can help save, restore, and heal the lives of veterans and their families. They can also help veterans follow through with applying for their benefits and advocating for needed resources. God used faith organizations of different religions and denominations to help my family and me. We were open to receiving the assistance and guidance. Veterans and their families deserve care. Fortunately, Scripture addresses their most common emotional needs. Scriptures and holy books as well as religious organizations "has answers when psychology alone has reached its limitations. A totally secular approach cannot begin to answer the problem of pain. From an atheist's or agnostic's perspective, suffering is dumb, capricious nonsense. Christianity and other religions have better answers as to why bad things happen to good people."[75]

---

[75] Waterhouse, Steven. *Strength for His People: A Ministry for Families of the Mentally Ill.* (Texas: Westcliff Press, 2002.), 70.

The Bible is full of scriptures that have helped me throughout my life. I have been inspired to live by faith and help veterans and their families by 2 Corinthians 1:3-5, which says: "Praise be to the God and Father of our Lord Jesus Christ, the Father of compassion and the God of all comfort, who comforts us in all our troubles, so that we can comfort those in any trouble with the comfort we ourselves receive from God."[76]

Writing this book was very difficult because it brought up so much pain for me. However, some healing has taken place during the process of finishing it. I dedicate this to all current military personnel, veterans, and their families, as well as to all the deceased who served their country. Your stories matter, and the contributions you

---

[76] 2 Corinthians 1:3-5

made to this nation were not in vain. Thank you for your sacrifices, dedication, and duty.

RESOURCES

Cranaleith Spiritual Center

13475 Proctor Road

Philadelphia, PA 19116

www.cranaleith.org

(215) 934-6206

Travis Manion Foundation

164 E. State Street

Doylestown, PA 18901

www.travismanion.org

(215) 348-9080

Women Veterans Alliance

69 Lincoln Blvd., Suite A306

Lincoln, CA 95648

www.womenveteransalliance.org

Women Veterans Rock

7782 Crittenden Street – Unit 27774

Philadelphia, PA 19118-0774

(215) 836-4262

Women Veterans Center

259 N. Lawrence Street

Philadelphia, PA 19106

www.vmcenter.org

(215) 644-3215

Veterans Crisis Line

(800) 273-8255

Vet to Vet Assistance

(888) 777-4443

Jewish War Veterans "Women in Military Life" on YouTube

Bibliography

Browder, Laura. *When Janey Comes Marching Home: Portraits of Women Combat Veterans.* North Carolina: University of North Carolina Press, 2010.

Carter, B and McGoldrick M. *The Expansive Family Life Cycle: Individual, Family, and Social Perspectives, 4th ed.* New York: Allyn & Bacon, 2010.

Chittister, Joan D. *Scarred by Struggle, Transformed by Hope.* Michigan: William B. Eerdmans Publishing Company, 2003.

Guerin, Dava and Kevin Ferris. *Unbreakable Bonds: The Mighty Moms and Wounded Warriors of Walter Reed.* New York: Skyhorse, 2014.

Holmstedt, Kirsten. *Band of Sisters: American Women at War in Iraq.* Pennsylvania: Stackpole Books, 2007.

Johnson, Shoshana and M. L. Doyle. *I'm Still Standing: From Captive U.S. Soldier to Free Citizen- My Journey Home.* New York: Simon & Schuster, 2010.

Kornfeld, M.Z., *Cultivating Wholeness: A Guide to Care and Counseling in Faith Communities.* New York: Continuum, 2000.

Maring, Norman H., and Winthrop S. Hudson. *A Baptist Manual of Polity and Practice*. Rev. ed. Valley Forge: Judson Press, 1991.

Seahorn, Janet J. and E. Anthony Seahorn. *Tears of a Warrior: A Family's Story of Combat and Living with PTSD*. Colorado: Team Pursuits, 2008.

Schneider, Eugene William III. "Practical Pastoral Care: Observations from a Military Chaplain in Dealing with Trauma" PhD dissertation, Lutheran Theological Seminary Philadelphia, 2009.

Sippola, John, Amy Blumenshine, Donald A. Tubesing, and Valerie Yancey. *Welcome Them Home Help Them Heal: Pastoral Care and Ministry with Service Members Returning from War*. Minnesota: Whole Person Associates, 2009.

Swain, Storm. *The T. Mort Chaplaincy at Ground Zero: Presence and Privilege on Holy Ground*. New York: Springer Publishing Company, 2011.

The Holy Bible, New International Version. Grand Rapids: Zondervan Publishing House, 1984.

Tick, Edward. *War and the Soul: Healing Our Nation's Veterans from Post-traumatic Stress Disorder*. Illinois: Theosophical Publishing House, 2005.

Tick, Edward, *Warrior's Return: Restoring the Soul After War*. Colorado: Sounds True, 2014.

Waterhouse, Steven. *Strength for His People: A Ministry for Families of the Mentally Ill*. Texas: Westcliff Press, 2002.

ABOUT THE AUTHOR

Constance C. Cotton is a retired war veteran that served as a reservist and active duty soldier in the U.S. Army. She is a graduate of The Lutheran Theological Seminary at Philadelphia. Coupled with her seminary training and her personal life experiences, Constance was directed to launch a ministry that caters to helping veterans and their families gain proper access to military benefits and resources. Constance is a trained service officer with the

VFW. She is a member of the American Veterans (AMVETS) and a lifetime member with the Disabled American Veterans (DAV). Constance is married with two sons and resides in New Jersey.

Made in the
USA
Middletown, DE